Everything
you need to know
to raise the perfect pup

Puppy School

Maggie Holt and Stella Sweeting

RODALE

WE **INSPIRE** AND **ENABLE** PEOPLE TO IMPROVE
THEIR LIVES AND THE WORLD AROUND THEM

A QUINTET BOOK

Published by Rodale, Inc.
33 East Minor Street,
Emmaus, PA 18098-0099

Library of Congress Cataloging-in-Publication Data

Holt, Maggie.
    Puppy school: everything you need to know to raise
the perfect pup / Maggie Holt and Stella Sweeting.
        p.   cm.
    "A Quintet Book."
    Includes index.
    ISBN 1–57954–915–2 paperback
    1. Dogs—Training. 2. Puppies—Training.
    I. Sweeting, Stella. II. Title.
    SF431.H793 2004
    636.7`0887—dc22   2003025445

This book was designed and produced by
Quintet Publishing Limited
6 Blundell Street
London N7 9BH

Contributing Editors: Charlene Dobson and
Richard Emerson
Senior Project Editor: Corinne Masciocchi
Associate Publisher: Laura Price
Designer: Ian Hunt
Photographer: Jeremy Thomas
Creative Director: Richard Dewing
Publisher: Oliver Salzmann

Manufactured in Singapore by
Universal Graphics Pte Limited
Printed in China by
Midas Printing International Limited

ACKNOWLEDGMENTS

With special thanks to all participating owners and
their dogs: Mike Abbs, his daughter Michaela, and
Weimaraner, Scooby; Sheila Baker and Pembrokeshire
Welsh corgi, Thomas; Cindy Cole and Hungarian
wirehaired vyzsla, Camber; Sue Fay and Labrador
retriever, Saffy; Val Funnel and Jack Russell terrier,
Jessie; Dawn Hassan and Staffordshire terrier, Moe;
Maggie Holt and Siberian husky, Xara; Jean McQuillan
and golden retriever, Cassis; Ann Miles and golden
retriever, Cassie; Mary Powderham and golden retriever,
Daisy; Janet Plimmer and Hungarian vyzsla, Hovis; Tim
Reed and Siberian husky, Lysack; Elizabeth Shepherd
and boxer, Lottie; Janet Smith, grandson Rohan May-
Smith, and mongrel, Sam; Jane Spencer-Butler and
Weimaraner, Aggie; Lucy Stevens and Weimaraner, Oscar;
Sue Stirling and cocker spaniels, Oscar and Henry; Stella
Sweeting and greyhound, Kylie; Valerie Tranter and
poodle, Ozy; Ian Tulloch and rough collie, Paddi

Also with thanks to: Veterinary surgeon Mark Johnston
and veterinary nurses Gayle, Suzie, and Rachel

Dedication to Sue
We are especially indebted to Sue Fay and her Labrador
retriever, Saffy, who played very important roles in the
writing and completion of this book. Saffy is featured
in many of the photos. Their help and support were
invaluable. We couldn't have done it without them!

Picture Credits
David Dalton, 124; Marc Henrie, 27; Carol Ann
Johnson, 6, 8, 14, 22b, 23t, 26, 33b, 37, 57, 60,
61, 70, 72t, 77, 135t; Sally Anne Thompson, 11,
15, 19, 21t, 23b, 35, 36, 38, 39, 54, 56b, 95, 128;
R. Willbie, 20t, 22t, 44, 132; The Kennel Club, 16,
34, 45, 73, 106, 135b, 136, 138, 141t; Quarto
Publishing, 20b, 21b, 24l, 24r, 25l, 25r, 28, 29, 30,
31, 59, 67.

RODALE
WE INSPIRE AND ENABLE PEOPLE TO IMPROVE
THEIR LIVES AND THE WORLD AROUND THEM

 Contents

1  What to expect

Among the many misconceptions about dog training is the belief that puppies should be taught discipline through the use of punishment. In this book we follow a different approach, one that does not involve punishment for "mistakes" or "bad behavior." Instead, we have found that it is far more beneficial and effective to reward the correct behavior. This approach will enable you to build the right relationship with your puppy because it involves understanding the way dogs think. Our methods show how to interpret your puppy's behavior, so that you can give him the proper training that he needs to become an obedient, responsive, and happy adult dog.

Decide carefully about house rules, and then be clear and consistent. This is especially important when it comes to whether or not puppy is allowed on your furniture!

The key to a happy, well-behaved dog is regular, consistent, systematic puppy training. By devoting time on a daily basis to your puppy's training, he will grow into a well-behaved, obedient, contented dog that is a pleasure to own. Poor or inadequate training, on the other hand, can lead to behavioral problems—such as willfulness, disobedience, moodiness, or aggression—that can be extremely disruptive to family life. The reward-based training methods explained in this book are non-punitive—they do not rely on punishment to get your puppy to learn. They are highly effective primarily because they take into account canine psychology—that is, the way dogs think.

Many behavioral problems concerning dogs come about not because of some innate "wickedness" on the part of the dog but because the owners have failed to understand the fundamentals of canine psychology. All dogs are, at heart, pack animals that need to conform to a strict social hierarchy within their group. The modern domesticated dog lives in a mixed canine/human family, but he still retains his social instincts and quickly learns to recognize his place in the family, or pack, hierarchy.

A puppy inherently wants to follow "the rules" of the pack and to keep to his place. In the wild, puppies do not need to be bullied into conforming by other pack members. The rewards that come from being in a pack are sufficient incentive in themselves. These rewards are: a sense of belonging, security from danger, the affection and companionship of the other members of the pack, a place to sleep, and a regular supply of good food. Puppies just need to learn what the rules are. This is true of the domestic canine/human "pack," too.

Establishing the right relationship with your puppy is as important as teaching your puppy basic obedience. It may seem an obvious thing to say, but your puppy does not speak English. Yet, even though we know that, we often expect puppies to understand us. Canines belong to a different species with a different way of thinking. Because of our close relationship with dogs, we like to imagine they think and react as we do, but they don't. If your pup is behaving in a way that you might describe as "being naughty," it is probably because he's behaving like a canine and hasn't understood what you want. Shouting at him and—far worse—hitting him, won't help him to understand what you require of him. He won't know what the problem is, and all you will teach him is that you are not to be trusted because you become aggressive for no reason.

To a dog there is no such thing as right and wrong—just canine instinct. It is unreasonable to expect a dog to understand our concept of right and wrong because he can't—it's as simple as that. So it is our responsibility to find ways to teach him what we require. Decide your house rules and work out how best to teach them to your puppy. Unless you teach him, he will not know the difference between acceptable and unacceptable behavior.

Always be consistent

Give your puppy clear, consistent house rules. If on one occasion you allow the pup to get onto your best armchair—because he looks so cute sleeping there and he's not doing any harm—then the next day you shout and scream at him for doing the same thing, because this time it's a wet day and your best armchair is now smothered in mud—you are being very inconsistent. It is unreasonable to expect the pup to understand when he is allowed on the chair and when he isn't. If you decide your puppy is allowed on the furniture then, if he is wet or muddy, don't let him have access to a chair until he is dry. BUT, if you do allow him on the furniture, make sure you teach him that he must get off if you tell him. If you have a problem getting him to jump off when you want him off, then it is best to make it a rule that he is not allowed on the furniture at all.

Food: Yours, not his

It is important for your relationship with your puppy that he respects your eating times. When you are sitting down to eat, never feed your pup scraps from the table. Some people think giving their dog these "extras" will make him love them more. Not so. Quite the reverse, in fact. If you are in the habit of sometimes eating food off a low table or TV tray, then continue this habit once the pup arrives. It is good for his discipline and very easy to teach him that this is your food and he is not to touch it. Usually a stare, or sometimes a growl or words said in a "growly" voice will suffice. On rare occasions you may even need to push him away gently, if the pup is very persistent. However, remember that dogs are opportunists and natural scavengers, so don't leave the food unattended at a low level. It would be very foolish to expect the pup not to take the opportunity literally handed to him on a plate! If he learns to steal, it's your fault for having left food unattended where he can reach it.

Never feed your puppy morsels of food from the dinner table, or he'll become a pest every single time you sit down to eat.

If you stay with your puppy while he is eating, it will help him to relax and trust you around his food.

Dinner time

Still on the subject of food, we can also affect our relationship with our pup by what we do at his feeding time. Some people seem to think it is necessary to give the dog his dinner and almost immediately remove the bowl, just to prove they can take it away. Then, when the dog growls, they adopt the "No dog's gonna growl at me!" attitude. If you just think about this from your viewpoint, you can see that it is an unreasonable thing to do. If someone put a plate of delicious food in front of you and almost immediately removed it, wouldn't you at least say, "Hey, what do you think you're doing?" Well, that's exactly what the dog is doing in the only way he knows how—by growling. This has nothing to do with rank or dominance. This is really about survival.

There are much easier ways to make sure your puppy is relaxed about his food bowl, provided you start as soon as the pup arrives in your home. If there are children in the family, they can do this too:

▌ Stay with him while he's eating—don't put the bowl down and leave the room.

▌ Without taking it away, handle the bowl while he is eating. Sometimes talk to him quietly, and very calmly and gently stroke him.

▌ Occasionally, put only part of his dinner in the bowl and, while he is still eating, gradually add some more food.

If you then need to remove the bowl for some reason, there will be no problem, because he has learned to trust you around his food.

Scolding your pup

There may be rare occasions when you will need to scold your puppy, but make sure you are always fair. The dog (puppy or adult) has an associative memory of only about three seconds. So, in order to associate a reprimand with an act, it has to come within three seconds of the misdemeanor. For example, if your pup chews the priceless Persian rug while you are out, there is no point in scolding him when you get home. He will have no idea why you are so angry, and all you will teach him is that you become aggressive for no reason and are not to be trusted. You were the one at fault for leaving the pup where he had access to something valuable.

The dog is a highly aurally and visually orientated animal, so he quickly notices anything "odd" about you, such as your tone of voice, body language, and mood. If your voice is angry or he reads anger in your body language, then he is likely to adopt an appeasing body posture, which is often misread as guilt and punished accordingly. Please don't fall into the trap of misunderstanding your puppy in this way—it will spoil your relationship. The only time it is reasonable to scold your puppy is if you have caught him in the act of doing something you don't want him to do. Tell him off in a growly voice and as soon as he stops whatever it is, change your attitude and your tone of voice. Never reprimand more than three seconds after the event.

If you are always consistent and fair to your puppy so that he knows he can trust you, he will feel secure and relaxed and will be much easier to train. Conversely, if your puppy learns that you cannot be trusted, he will be insecure, tense,

and anxious, and training him will be much more difficult. So be fair to your puppy! It makes for a better life for you both!

Learning through play

The dog pack hierarchy is mainly established through play, and we should remember this when we play games with our puppies. Young puppies learn a tremendous amount from each other through playing together. It begins when they are siblings in the litter and continues when puppies meet up at puppy school. Through play, they learn about "bite inhibition"—that is, the ability to control the biting instinct; they discover how to manipulate each other; they continue to learn about how the pecking order is established; and they also learn about the calming signals (canine body language) so necessary to ensure good relationships and avoid conflict with the other puppies and dogs they will meet during their life.

In puppy school, pups come from different backgrounds and initially don't know each other,

Through play, puppies learn the social structure and body language signals of canine behavior, which are necessary for good relationships with other dogs.

so it is important that play times are properly supervised. Without this supervision (and—sometimes—intervention), it is only too easy for a confident, boisterous pup to turn into a bully, or for a shy, insecure pup to decide that play with his own species is no fun, possibly making him more shy, nervous, and/or aggressive.

With proper supervision, a confident, boisterous pup will realize that his "crash, bang, wallop" approach brings no reward, and he will try different, calmer tactics in order to achieve what he wants: to have fun playing. And, because of the calmer approach, the shy puppy gains confidence to play.

In the same way, your puppy will learn a tremendous amount by playing with you. It is best not to play rough-and-tumble, wrestling-type games with dogs of any age, as it tends to give them the wrong idea of their status. It is far better to play games that make the pup use his brain rather than his brawn—such as hide and seek, and fetch.

Tug o' war-type games with a toy are also best avoided until the pup has learned complete bite inhibition. Even then, it is important that you win the game and trophy the toy more times than your pup, otherwise, again, you could give him the wrong idea about his status.

Manipulation

Like most animals, including humans, puppies and dogs quickly learn to manipulate their environment to their advantage, so try to make sure that, in your relationship with your puppy, you are the one who gives the lead and makes the decisions. If you play with your puppy every time he pushes a toy at you, you are teaching him that he can get you to play whenever he wants. Play with your puppy often, but make sure that most of the time it is at your instigation, not at the demand of your pup.

The same applies to attention. If every time your pup comes up and nudges your arm for attention, and you oblige him, you are teaching

Give your puppy lots of attention, but make sure it's on your terms, so that he is not confused about his status.

him that he can get your attention whenever he likes. Give your puppy lots of attention and fussing, but make sure that most of the time it is at your instigation, not his.

Praise that puppy!

Make sure that you let your puppy know, on a regular basis, when he is doing something right. If he is just lying down quietly, tell him, in a quiet, calm voice, what a good dog he is. He won't understand the words, but he will understand the praising tone. If you let him know you are pleased with what he is doing, not only will the behavior you want occur more often, but it will help him to feel more relaxed and secure.

Rewards

When teaching your puppy how to behave, the type of reward you give is likely to vary according to the circumstances and, sometimes, according to the temperament of the puppy. Some rewards, such as a treat, or verbal praise, involve little physical contact. Others involve a lot of physical contact in the form of fussing and petting—in other words, stroking your puppy and being generally affectionate toward him. If your puppy is very excitable, then praise and physical contact will usually need to be much lower-key than if you have a more placid puppy.

The type of relationship you have with your puppy will affect all aspects of his life, including how well he is able to learn from you when you try to teach him obedience exercises. The human needs to be the pack leader. However, within the hierarchy of the dog or wolf pack, the pack leader rules with a benevolent authority, not a punitive regime. We need to do the same. As you will see, punishment does not play any part in our training methods. A puppy will learn much more quickly if he is praised and rewarded for doing right, rather than punished for doing

Reward your puppy's good behavior with treats and lots of praise. Give some extra treats and praise when he has done exceptionally well.

wrong. In this book, we have recipes for "puppy treats" that your dog will love. Give a treat and lots of praise whenever your puppy has behaved well and followed the rules, and give extra treats and praise when he has behaved especially well.

The time and effort you put in now, during the puppy's early, formative months, will quickly pay dividends. Very soon you will have a highly responsive puppy who is eager to learn and to earn your praise—a pet who is a joy to own and a pleasure to take with you whenever you visit friends and neighbors. Perhaps more importantly, he will grow into an adult dog who is well behaved and responsive to commands, not out of fear but out of choice, because he is happy, contented, secure, and—above all—he knows the rules.

Maggie Holt and Stella Sweeting

2 What to consider first

Most families gleefully welcome puppies as delightful and amusing new additions to the household. Often a great deal of affection is lavished upon the endearing newcomer, but what happens when the novelty wears off and the demands of raising a puppy become increasingly taxing? Buying a puppy requires a great deal of serious consideration regarding the commitment involved in rearing a well-adjusted dog. In this chapter, we explore the issues to take into account when deciding whether to get a puppy. These include factors such as your family members, where you live, the amount of time and money you can afford, and choosing the right breed to match both your preferences and your lifestyle.

Choosing a breed

A PUPPY REPRESENTS A MAJOR COMMITMENT IN TERMS OF TIME, MONEY AND, OF COURSE, LOVE. BEFORE YOU COMMIT YOURSELF TO OWNING A PUPPY, YOU OWE IT TO YOURSELF, YOUR FAMILY, AND, ABOVE ALL, ANY PUPPY YOU MIGHT BUY TO MAKE SURE YOU ARE MAKING THE RIGHT DECISION.

Buying a puppy must be a joint decision for the whole family. Remember, the presence of the pup (and the adult dog he'll become) will affect every one of you. Everyone in the family should share responsibility for the puppy's daily care, such as feeding, walking, grooming, and training. Don't buy a puppy just for the children's sake. If they grow tired of the pup, it may be busy Mom, who may never have wanted a dog in the first place, who is forced to look after it.

Another issue to consider is the family demographics: age and number of children, any elderly family members or visitors, and any existing dogs or other pets you may have. For example, a puppy may not be suitable if you have very young children. You must decide when you think a child is old enough to cope with a boisterous young dog and can appreciate that a puppy is not a toy and will not always want to play.

Puppies are cute and cuddly, but many mature into large dogs that require a great deal of mental and physical stimulation. Make sure you can handle the responsibility.

A lively young collie would probably not be suitable for elderly people, but could be fine for older children or a couple with time and energy to devote to his training. If you have other pets, such as a cat or a rabbit, that the puppy is unfamiliar with, they will need very careful introduction (*see* page 38).

Where do you live?

Consider whether you have sufficient space for a dog of the breed you want. No matter how cute and cuddly the puppy looks at the moment, he will grow into an adult that will need plenty of room to move around in and to exercise. Therefore the type of environment in which you live is important. Do you live in an apartment or a house, in a city, suburb, or rural area? Do you have easy access to parks, woods, beaches, or other open spaces where dogs are allowed? Most breeds adapt to town or country living, but certain hunting dogs, such as the American water spaniel and bloodhound, and working dogs are more suited to rural locations.

Think about potential difficulties caused by the layout of your house and grounds. Is there direct access to a yard and, if so, how big is it? Even though large breeds can curl up in small spaces indoors, all dogs need outside access. The balcony of an apartment may be acceptable for small toy breeds, but not, for example, a German shepherd. Does the front door open directly onto the road? Is the yard secure, or could an adventurous puppy escape? Problems like these can often be solved with a little foresight (*see* page 40).

How much time do you have?

Another important factor is the amount of time you and your family can devote to the puppy. For example, do you work full-time or part-time, every day or just some days? If you and/or your

If you have young children, consider whether they could cope with a boisterous young pup.

partner's work takes you away from home during the day, would anyone else be around to care for the dog? Puppies need constant attention, and even adult dogs should not be kept on their own for too long. Remember, unlike cats, dogs are highly social animals and can become distressed if abandoned for long periods. Four hours is about the limit most dogs should be left alone.

How much will dog-owning cost?

You should also think about how much money you have to spend. You can pay out a lot of money for a puppy, especially for a pedigree dog. And the bills don't end there. Food, toys, bedding and other equipment, veterinary care, insurance, and arrangements for vacations, if the dog needs to be left in kennels during your absence, must all be taken into account. The costs soon mount up. As a general rule, the bigger the dog and the more specialized the breed, the greater the financial outlay.

What's the best age?

The best age to take a puppy home is around ten weeks old, or just before, when it is starting to become more independent but can still adapt easily to a new environment. What happens during the puppy's first ten weeks is likely to have a permanent effect on the pup. Puppies learn a lot about life and how to behave from their mother and their littermates (see page 19). Removing them from that environment too soon can deprive them of an important education.

From five to twelve weeks is the "critical socialization period," when a pup learns how to respond to other dogs and people. At ten weeks, provided the puppy was raised by a responsible and knowledgeable breeder, he has had the best possible start in life, and there are still two weeks of the important socialization period left so you can go out and about with the pup, encountering all the things the pup will have to cope with in the human world, visiting friends and family, and continuing to expose the pup to people of all ages and descriptions (see page 108). This is also the best time for a puppy to settle into the domestic setting and bond with his new family before he becomes too set in his ways. If the vaccination program is not complete, the pup will have to be carried in public places to avoid contact.

Before eight weeks, puppies are not fully weaned, so they rely on their mothers for food as well as emotional support. Puppies over twelve weeks are likely to have formed strong associations to their home and may find it difficult to adjust to a new environment. By this time, puppies may even be starting to develop unwanted behavioral traits that will become increasingly difficult to train out again.

Male or female?

You should give some thought to the sex of the puppy—there are pros and cons to both genders. As a general rule, males tend to be more independent than females, so they can be more difficult to train. Unless they're neutered, they will follow a bitch in "season" (that is, fertile) for miles, given the opportunity. Females tend to be more responsive and flexible, so they can be easier to train. However, unless they're spayed (neutered), they come into season for three weeks twice a year, when they will attract unwanted

Ten weeks is the best age to bring a puppy home; he will find it easier to settle into his new family and surroundings.

THE FEAR IMPRINT PERIOD

Before ten weeks is a bad time to take a puppy away from his mother and siblings and put him in a strange environment. Around the age of eight weeks, puppies pass through a stage of development known as the first "fear imprint period," when any unpleasant or frightening occurrence can have a lasting effect (see page 138). Puppies are very vulnerable at this stage of their development, so life should be kept stable, secure, and normal at this time. It is also important that any potentially frightening experience, including elective surgery such as dew claw removal or treatment for hernia, be avoided at this time. Any traumatic event at this stage can result in lasting fears and phobias that are difficult or impossible to eradicate. At this time, visits to a vet should be as positive as possible.

Many breeders interrupt the normal weaning process by removing the mother from her pups for ever-increasing periods. They do this to dry up her milk, so they can sell the pups by the time they are eight weeks old. Yet this is a critical period in the social development of the puppies. At around eight weeks, the relationship of the pups to each other and to their mother begins to change. Mom will start to play with and discipline her offspring, and thereby teach the pups important lessons. A good canine mother is very wise. She will focus on those pups she recognizes as being too "pushy" and teach them how to control their behavior. Pups that miss out on this important stage in their education, especially the more assertive ones, are likely to be far less amenable to human discipline, and may even react aggressively to it. At this time, play with siblings becomes rougher, and learning "bite inhibition"—when, and when not to, use their teeth and jaws—becomes an important issue between pups. If one pup hurts another, the "victim" retaliates angrily, and the offender will normally back down without retaliation. They will continue the game as though nothing had happened, except that play will not be quite so rough. This type of learning helps when the pups' eventual owners continue to teach them about "bite inhibition" (*see page 73*).

attention from males. It is very important that females be kept secure at these times— amounting to around six weeks a year, in total—if you want to avoid the risk of unwanted litters. If you don't intend to breed from your dog, another option is to have him or her neutered, which will solve many of these problems.

What is the right breed for you?

Once you've made up your mind to buy, the next question is: What sort of dog should I choose? Think about where you live—town, city, suburb, homestead—and how much space you'll have for the puppy to run around in. And don't forget, puppies don't stay cute and adorable forever, so plan ahead and give some thought to how you'll cope with the adult dog once he is fully grown. It goes without saying that the bigger the breed, the more space you'll need. (So an Irish wolfhound is probably unsuitable if you live in a small apartment or have limited outdoor space in which the dog can move about freely.)

Temperament and lifestyle—yours and his

Consider your temperament and lifestyle, things such as your hobbies and leisure activities. Do you enjoy walking, riding or fishing, or do you prefer regular visits to the movies, theater or restaurants? Whatever your interests, would the dog be able to enjoy them with you? If you are physically very active and outgoing, you may want a dog that can, for example, go running or hiking with you, keep up with your bicycle, or just accompany you when you jog round the park. If so, a good choice is a medium-size breed traditionally used for herding or sporting work, such as a Springer spaniel. Their body shape is ideal for constant running. For young couples who enjoy long hikes in the woods, a strong and active breed such as a Labrador may be suitable.

If you are buying a dog for your children, choose a breed that is quick and eager to learn tricks and play games. On the other hand, if you are the quiet, introspective type, you might prefer a placid breed that is content to lie at

If you are physically active and outgoing, you may want a dog that can go running or hiking with you, keep up with your bicycle, or just accompany you when you jog in the park.

your feet while you watch TV, read a book or listen to music. Remember, too, that with care and attention, your dog may live to be over 14 years old, so, when choosing a dog, think about future aims and likely lifestyle, and don't just plan for the present.

Another factor to consider when choosing a breed is climate. A thick coat provides a dog with excellent insulation—a useful characteristic if you live in a cold climate—but in warmer climates, the dog may often need to stop and rest in order to cool down. Bear in mind that breeds with thick, shaggy or curly coats will need daily grooming and regular careful clipping to remove knots and avoid matting. A smooth, fine coat, on the other hand, needs less grooming and allows the dog to lose heat more quickly. However, you may need to put a dog coat on him in cold and wet weather.

Mixed-breed dogs

Unless you have set your heart on a purebred dog, it is worth considering mongrels (mutts) and crossbreeds. A mongrel is a mixture of several breeds. They are often highly intelligent and can make very good family dogs. They can be highly individual in shape, coloring, and temperament. However, unless one breed seems to predominate in the puppy, you cannot be sure exactly what kind of dog he will grow into, or how big he'll become. Purebred dogs can be very expensive,

Gun dogs like this German pointer are good-tempered and easy to train, which makes them ideal household pets, especially for families with children, although they do need regular exercise and lots of space.

which makes mongrels a much more affordable alternative, especially for families.

A crossbred dog can offer a good compromise between purebred and mongrel. A crossbreed is the first cross from two purebred dogs, such as a cock-a-poo, a cocker spaniel–poodle cross. By mixing two breeds, you can often get the best characteristics from the two—perhaps strength and agility from one breed and loyalty and intelligence from the other. (Bear in mind, though, you can also get the worst traits from the two breeds!)

Purebred dogs

Purebred dogs have usually been selectively bred for a particular purpose. So, before you buy one, think long and hard about the reason why a particular breed looks like that and whether it will be suitable for your needs. If you don't know the origin of a particular breed, find out as much about it as you can by checking out your local library, or the internet, or by contacting the various breed societies.

Most breeds were produced for work, hunting/sport, or as show or companion dogs. For example, border collies were bred for herding sheep, hounds were selected to track animals such as deer or foxes, and gun dogs were designed to fetch game birds that had been shot down. The dog will still carry those traits, so

Lively sporting breeds like cocker spaniels need owners that are energetic and active. Their thick coats also require regular grooming.

Adaptable, affectionate, and loyal, racing dogs like this greyhound enjoy short bursts of speed, but are otherwise content to laze around, which makes them great pets for families with large yards.

Intelligent and lively breeds enjoy lots of exercise, becoming very popular as family dogs.

Show dogs have been selected mainly on the basis of their appearance rather than their behavioral traits. So, if looks are most important, go to a show breeder or general breeder. However, for a working or sporting dog, go to a specialist breeder, who will have selected strains that show an aptitude for the particular task. Bear in mind, too, that working dogs such as collies, or sporting dogs such as gun dogs, are bred to be highly active and intelligent, so they need to be kept physically and mentally occupied. The following examples should help you to know what to expect from a particular breed. But remember, there are always exceptions, and all dogs are individuals, so you must not assume that the puppy you buy will conform to character.

knowing what it was originally bred to do helps you to know what to expect. You can assume that retrievers, which were originally bred to be gun dogs, will be better at retrieving than greyhounds, for instance. Some dogs were bred to catch rabbits and other game, and you will find it difficult to get them to behave otherwise.

Sporting and hunting breeds

Hounds, such as beagles and foxhounds, were bred for hunting, either on their own or in packs, and you can see this innate behavior in the way they instinctively chase after other animals, often with other dogs. They were mostly expected to work independently of man, so they are not as

Gentle and good-natured non-sporting breeds such as the bichon frise make ideal pets for less active or elderly people and are also popular show dogs.

With their strong chasing instinct, hunting dogs such as these foxhounds can play or work for long periods of time.

responsive to commands—or as eager to please their owners—as other, more people-oriented breeds. As a consequence, they are not so good at playing games such as "run and fetch" and tackling an obstacle course. Unless you plan to make use of the hound's natural instincts and to put in the extra time to train him, the innate urge to hunt and chase could get your dog—and you—into a lot of trouble. The greyhound, in particular, is bred to chase a lure, meaning that it will instinctively chase and kill small animals, so be aware that this type of dog is not really suitable to have around smaller pets, such as rats or guinea pigs.

Many people do not realize that terriers were, originally, hunting dogs, trained to catch foxes

and to dig rats, mice, rabbits, and other prey from burrows in the ground. The desire to dig is still very strong in them. If you choose a terrier, don't be surprised if he demonstrates his skills on your prize lawn or flowerbed. Terriers retain their powerful hunting instinct, so, if they are not

Originally bred for hunting, terriers are active, playful, intelligent, and full of personality, making them ideal pets for extroverted older children.

DOGS WILL BE DOGS

Remember that all dogs will, on occasion, just act like dogs. They'll bark, dig, chase, and run around excitedly—regardless of breed. It is up to you to try to channel these behaviors into activities that are more socially acceptable.

properly trained and socialized, they can pose a threat to other pets and, sometimes, babies and small children. They can also be extremely strong-willed, so you need persistence and patience during training. On the plus side, their active and intelligent nature makes them ideal for outgoing older children, since they have lots of personality, boundless energy, and love playing games.

Some dogs, such as Staffordshire and bull terriers, originally bred for blood sports, have strong characters with independent natures that make them suitable for families with older children or teenagers. Gun dogs have been carefully bred to work closely with humans—to stalk prey, and then to run and fetch on command. This has made them highly intelligent and very active, so they are ideal for playful families. Golden retrievers and Labradors are usually placid, good-natured dogs, being friendly with the children of the house, as well as with any visiting play pals.

Working and herding breeds

Working dog breeds are naturally exuberant, so they need regular exercise—physical and mental—or they can become boisterous, difficult to control, and even destructive as they seek an outlet for their natural energy. This means that as the dog grows he will need plenty of exercise—including playing games and also learning new tricks—to keep him interested (*see* page 46).

Herding dogs, such as collies and shepherd dogs, were originally bred to corral sheep and other livestock by rounding up the animals, usually following commands. They are extremely fit and active, and have the strength and stamina to run around all day if necessary. If they do not find a normal outlet for their natural behavior they can channel it into undesirable activities, such as chasing bicycles, joggers, children playing ball, and other pets, such as cats. Choose breeds like this only if you are an experienced owner, and have a great deal of

Staffordshire terriers are strong natured, independent, and sturdy, so they are perfectly suited to families with older children or teenagers.

Both a working dog and a guard dog, the energetic and intelligent German shepherd needs an experienced owner who can provide the physical and mental stimulation that these breeds require.

Each year, hundreds of thousands of dogs arrive at rescue centers because their owners are no longer able—or prepared—to look after them. On average, about 25 percent are unwanted presents, another 25 percent have behavioral problems, and the rest are given up for domestic or other reasons. Here are some of the most common reasons:

1. The breed was that year's "must-have" accessory (the "101 Dalmatians" factor).
2. The cute fluffy little puppy was irresistible—but he didn't stay cute and little for long.
3. Due to lack of training, the dog got aggressive, destructive, or uncontrollable.
4. The dog was acquired on impulse, usually to please children, before the owners realized the level of commitment involved.
5. The dog was left alone for long periods, barking and upsetting the neighbors and/or becoming aggressive, destructive, or uncontrollable.
6. The elderly owners could no longer cope with the demands of dog ownership.
7. The expense of dog owning—feeding, neutering, veterinary treatment, boarding costs during vacation—got to be too much.
8. The marriage or relationship broke up and no one wanted the dog.
9. The overriding needs of a young family or the arrival of a new baby made dog ownership too difficult.
10. The owners moved to a new apartment with a "no pets" rule.

time and space so you will be able to keep your pet physically active and mentally occupied for long periods each day to provide a natural outlet for his energies.

Although border collies are bred to work closely with humans and follow instructions, many people find these breeds are not particularly biddable or easy to train in a domestic setting. German shepherds also tend to be highly strung and prone to temperament problems. One of the best pet breeds of working dog is the sheltie (Shetland sheepdog), an intelligent and affectionate breed that responds well to basic training. They are adaptable in the amount of exercise they require but, like all working dogs, need to be kept active. They enjoy playing games, so they make ideal dogs for families with older children. Although sometimes a rather nervous breed, the sheltie is not known for excessive barking—a bonus if you want to stay on good terms with your neighbors—but they will warn of approaching strangers.

The fit and active border collie was originally bred to round up livestock by following commands, so these herding dogs need a lot of space in which to run around.

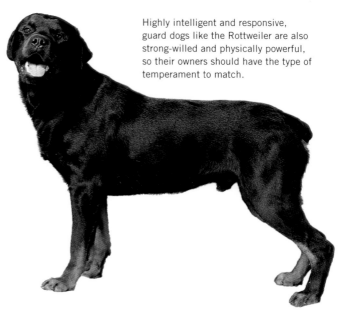

Highly intelligent and responsive, guard dogs like the Rottweiler are also strong-willed and physically powerful, so their owners should have the type of temperament to match.

Guard dogs

Many working dogs have a "guarding instinct," but some breeds, such as the Doberman and Rottweiler, were bred specifically as guard dogs. These breeds are highly intelligent and eager to learn, so they respond well to a regular, well-planned training program. However, they are also very large and powerful, which presents particular problems in terms of upkeep. They are also strong willed, so they will be a challenge unless their owners have a strong character, too. Remember: You are responsible for your dog's actions, so if you own a guard dog, you must ensure that he is well trained and does not pose a threat to your community.

Non-sporting and toy breeds

Less active people, especially the elderly and others with impaired mobility, may want a pet mainly for companionship. In this case, the best option might be a small breed that is not too active by nature and is content to fit in with your domestic routine. Toy and non-sporting breeds such as the bichon frise, miniature poodle, Maltese terrier, and Pomeranian have been bred to enjoy close contact with their owners. Loved for their affectionate and entertaining

If you plan to get a guard dog, it will be your responsibility to make sure that he receives proper training and does not become a nuisance to your neighborhood.

personalities, most companion dogs are also especially gentle and good natured. A small dog is less likely to cause injury to her owner by running around or jumping up during her early boisterous phase of puppyhood but could trip an elderly owner.

All dogs need regular exercise, but small companion dogs are content with short walks supplemented by simple games played in the house or yard that will tire out the dog, but not the owner. An ideal general family dog for first-time owners is the Cavalier King Charles spaniel. Easy to train, and not too big, this dog can cope with the rough and tumble of being around children but doesn't need to be kept constantly active, so they make good companion dogs.

Sporting dogs like these Welsh springer spaniels are full of energy and enjoy being part of the action, so they are perfectly suited to active people and outdoor life.

Dog breeds at a glance

THE FOLLOWING PAGES LIST THE BROADER CLASSIFICATIONS OF BREEDS WITHIN WHICH DIFFERENT TYPES OF DOGS ARE GROUPED—SPORTING AND HUNTING, WORKING AND HERDING, AND NON-SPORTING AND TOY BREEDS.

SPORTING AND HUNTING BREEDS

Gun dogs:

American Cocker Spaniel, American Water Spaniel, Bourbonnais Setter, Brittany Spaniel, Cavalier King Charles Spaniel, Chesapeake Bay Retriever, Clumber Spaniel, Curly-coated Retriever, Dupuy Setter, English Cocker Spaniel, English Setter, English Springer Spaniel, Field Spaniel, Flat-coated Retriever, French Setter, French Spaniel, German Pointer, German Spaniel, Golden Retriever, Gordon Setter, Hungarian Coarse-haired Vizsla, Hungarian Vizsla, Irish Red and White Setter, Irish Setter, Irish Water Spaniel, Italian Setter, Italian Spinone, Kooikerhondje, Labrador Retriever, Large and Small Münsterländers, Nova Scotia Duck Tolling Retriever, Pointer, Portuguese Setter, Pudelpointer, Saint-Germain Setter, Stabyhoun, Weimeraner, Welsh Springer Spaniel, Wire-haired Pointing Griffon

Cavalier King Charles Spaniel

Chesapeake Bay Retriever

Irish Setter

Italian Spinone

Hounds:

Afghan Hound, American Foxhound, Anglo-French, Ariègeois, Artois, Basenji, Basset, Beagle, Beagle Harrier, Billy, Black and Tan Coonhound, Borzoi, Briquet Griffon Vendéen, Dachsbrackes, Dachshunds, Deerhound, English Foxhound, French, Great Gascony Blue, Greyhound, Griffons Vendéen, Grand and Basset, Hamiltonstövare, Hanover, Harrier, Hungarian Greyhound, Ibizan, Irish Wolfhound, Italian Segugio, Jämthund, Jura, Nivernais Griffon, Otterhound, Petit Basset Griffon Vendéen, Pharaoh Hound, Poitevin, Porcelaine, Portuguese Podengo, Redbone Coonhound, Rhodesian Ridgeback, Saluki, Sicilian Hound, Sloughi, Spanish Greyhound, Swiss, Bernese and Lucernese Hounds, Tahltan Bear Dog, Tawny Brittany Basset, Whippet

Terriers:

Airedale, Australian, Bedlington, Border, Bull, Cairn, Czesky, Fox (Smooth and Wire), German Hunt, Harlequin Pinscher, Irish, Jack Russell, Japanese, Kerry Blue, Lakeland, Manchester, Norfolk, Norwich, Parson Russell, Scottish, Skye, Soft-coated Wheaten, Staffordshire, Welsh, West Highland White

Afghan Hound

Airedale Terrier

Rhodesian Ridgeback

Smooth Fox Terrier

WORKING AND HERDING BREEDS

Workers:
Ainu Dog, Alaskan Malamute, Bernese Mountain Dog, Boxer, Brazilian Guard, Bullmastiff, Canaan Dog, Doberman, Dogue de Bordeaux, Eskimo Dog, Estrela Mountain Dog, Eurasier, Great Dane, Greenland Dog, Hungarian Kuvasz, Japanese Akita, Japanese Fighting Dog, Komondor, Lapland Spitz, Leonberger, Mastiff, Mudi, Neapolitan Mastiff, Pinscher, Portuguese Water Dog, Pyrenean Mastiff, Pyrenean Mountain Dog, Rottweiler, Saint Bernard, Samoyed, Siberian Husky, Spanish Mastiff, Swedish Vallhund, Tibetan Mastiff

Herders:
Anatolian Shepherd, Appenzell Mountain, Australian Cattle, Australian Kelpie, Bearded Collie, Beauce Shepherd, Belgian Shepherd, Bergamasco, Bernese Mountain, Border Collie, Bouvier des Ardennes, Bouvier des Flandres, Briard, Dutch Shepherd, Entlebuch Mountain Dog, German Shepherd, Hovawart, Hungarian Puli, Lancashire Heeler, Lapponian Herder, Maremma Sheepdog, Newfoundland, Old English Sheepdog, Picardy Shepherd, Polish Lowland Sheepdog, Pumi, Pyrenean Shepherd, Rough Collie, Rumanian Shepherd, Russian Shepherd, Shetland Sheepdog, Smooth Collie, Welsh Corgi (Pembroke and Cardigan)

Bullmastiff

Bearded Collie

Bernese Mountain Dog

Saint Bernard

NON-SPORTING AND TOY BREEDS

Affenpinscher, Australian Silky Terrier, Bichon Frise, Bolognese, Boston Terrier, Brussels Griffon, Bulldog, Chihuahua, Chinese Crested Dog, Chow Chow, Coton de Tulear, Dalmatian, English Toy Terrier, Finnish Spitz, French Bulldog, German Spitz, Giant Schnauzer, Havanese, Italian Greyhound, Japanese Chin, Japanese Spitz, Keeshond, King Charles Spaniel, Lhasa Apso, Löwchen, Maltese, Mexican Hairless, Miniature Pinscher, Miniature Poodle, Miniature Schnauzer, Papillon, Pekingese, Pomeranian, Pug, Schipperke, Schnauzer, Shar-Pei, Shiba Inu, Shih Tzu, Standard Poodle, Tibetan Spaniel, Tibetan Terrier, Toy Poodle, Yorkshire Terrier

Miniature Schnauzer

Shih Tzu

Chihuahua

Dalmatian

Pug

Buying a puppy

ALWAYS SEEK OUT A REPUTABLE BREEDER WHO CARES ABOUT DOGS AS PETS AND COMPANIONS—NOT MERELY STOCK FOR BREEDING PURPOSES—AND HAS THEIR ANIMALS' WELFARE AT HEART. THE BREEDER YOU CHOOSE SHOULD BE A SOURCE OF INFORMATION AS WELL AS PUPPIES AND PROVIDE SUPPORT FOR YOU AS A FUTURE DOG OWNER.

Before you visit a dog breeder, think about the questions you will need to ask him or her. In particular, you should discuss with the breeder the characteristics of the chosen breed to make sure that they are compatible with your lifestyle and family circumstances (*see* page 16.) Bear in mind that a reputable breeder will also have questions for you. Just as you need to make sure that your puppy has come from a good home and is fit and healthy, the breeder will want to ensure that the puppy is going to a good home where he will be loved and well cared for. Responsible breeders should refuse to sell puppies to people they think would make unsuitable owners.

If you are choosing a mixed-breed dog, go to a good rescue center in your neighborhood or ask dog-owning friends or colleagues whose opinion you value. Avoid buying in response to newspaper advertisements or from pet shops. If you are considering buying a pedigree puppy, you can obtain a list of licensed breeders in your area from the relevant breed society. You will be able to find the address of their main office on the internet, or there may be a local branch of the society advertising in your town newspaper. (Before buying a purebred puppy, you will need confirmation that the litter was registered with the relevant organization and that the official papers are available.) You could also visit dog shows, where you can obtain information about

dog breeders and observe your chosen breed first hand. Local veterinary offices provide another possible source of advice and information. Avoid puppy farms, where the dogs are often kept in inhumane conditions.

Questions for your breeder

Is the puppy socialized?

Ask the breeder to explain how the litter has been socialized with people as well as dogs. Puppies' early experiences have such an effect on their future that this socialization is vital if they are to develop into confident adults. For example, have they met other animals, such as cats and rabbits? Are they used to being handled and played with? And if so, by whom? Have they become accustomed to visitors, including children, or have they only met the breeder and his or her immediate family? You will also need to ask at what age the breeder is willing to allow the puppy to go to a new home. The best age is ten weeks (*see* page 18.)

Is he used to a variety of noises?

You should try to find out where the litter has been kept. Have they been penned outside or inside the house? Many subsequent behavior problems will be avoided if puppies have had early exposure to normal household sounds.

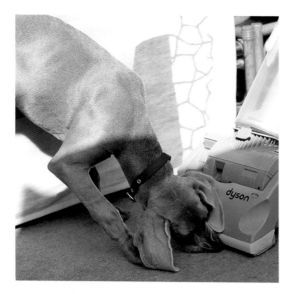

Puppies need to be familiar with the different sights and sounds of their new home environment, especially things like the vacuum cleaner, which could confuse or startle any newcomer!

For example, you should make sure that they have become accustomed to the routine of the family and the house and its sounds. Puppies need to be familiar with things such as the vacuum cleaner, the refrigerator, the telephone and doorbell ringing, the radio and television, people talking, and so on.

What's the puppy's medical history?

Perhaps the most critical question to ask is about the puppy's medical history. You should expect to receive proof that the relevant tests have been carried out and that the results were satisfactory. For example, has the mother or the litter experienced any medical problems? Was the birth normal? Have the parents been tested for hereditary defects such as hip dysplasia (joint abnormality) and eye disorders? Has the breeder started the puppies' worming program and routine vaccinations, and if so, when? You should ask the breeder for written information about the puppy's diet, which, to avoid health problems such as stomach upset, you should not change in the initial stages.

What to look for at the breeder's

You should expect to see the litter with their mother. By observing the mother, her reactions to you—as a stranger—and the way she interacts with her puppies, you should be able to gain an impression of her temperament, and therefore an idea of how the puppies' personalities may develop. A steady, calm, reliable, and contented mother is a good sign that she is physically well

The mother's interaction with her litter will tell you a lot about her emotional as well as her physical condition—a good indication of what the puppies may be like.

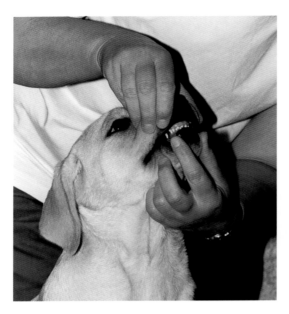

Conduct a thorough physical examination of any puppy you're interested in, so that you can detect any signs of infection or disease.

The puppy's coat should be glossy without being oily. Watch out for flakes of skin or loose hairs, especially after stroking. In "wrinkly" breeds, check in the folds of skin for signs of inflammation, irritation, or scabs. Check for redness and discharge, especially from the eyes and ears. The whites of the eyes should be clear, bright, and shiny, and the eyelids should be clean. The ears should be a healthy pink, and there should be no odor or waxy discharge. Gently part the puppy's jaws to look in the mouth and check that the gums are pink and free of odor. The anal area should be clean and dry and free from signs of diarrhea or discharge.

You can judge the puppies' temperament by how they react to being handled. Puppies that take an interest in you and in their surroundings are likely to be alert and intelligent. They're showing the signs of developing confidence. An ideal pet dog should be neither overly shy or fearful nor too boisterous. A timid puppy can often grow up into a shy and fearful adult,

and emotionally well adjusted, so you can hope to see the same traits in her offspring. Ideally, you should ask to see the father as well, to ensure that he shares these characteristics, although this may not always be practical, since many breeders don't own the fathers and they may live far away. Having met the parents, you should also have some idea of the puppy's eventual size as an adult.

Take the opportunity to handle all the puppies one by one. This will allow you to judge their health and temperament. Examine the puppies closely to check their physical condition. A healthy, well-fed puppy feels solid and surprisingly heavy, with firm muscles and straight sturdy limbs. In a young puppy, any signs of redness, discharge, or unpleasant smells should ring warning bells in your mind. Not only are these signs of infection or inflammation, but they indicate that the puppy may not have been well looked after.

HALLMARKS OF A GOOD BREEDER

Look for these signs of a good breeder:
- There is plenty of good quality food for mom and for the pups when they're weaned.
- The pups have access to plenty of fresh air and sunshine.
- The mother is kept with the pups and not removed for long periods of time.
- The pups are reared in the home where they can hear and see all the aspects of a typical household routine that they are likely to encounter in their new home.
- The pups are regularly and affectionately handled by the breeder and family.
- The pups receive regular visitors of all ages who handle and play with them.
- Where the breeder has other adult dogs, the pups have plenty of opportunity to meet with and learn from those adults that enjoy their company. (Some adult dogs are not happy around puppies—the knowledgeable breeder will be well aware of this.)

which will not make a good pet, especially if you have a family. The shy dog will find it hard to socialize, both with humans and other dogs, and could find life in a family stressful. Nervousness is a common cause of aggression, so the dog might resort to biting if he's afraid. Beware of overconfidence in a puppy, however, as this can show an overly assertive nature, and may mean the puppy will be difficult to train. Although obedience can be established through training and good relationships with the owner, it will be much easier if the dog's nature is not too assertive in the first place.

Questions the breeder may ask you

Finally, you should expect the breeder to have plenty of questions for you, and you should worry if he didn't, since it would suggest that the breeder did not care about the home the puppy was going to. The first question that the breeder is likely to ask you is whether you have kept dogs before and, if so, whether you had ever owned dogs of this particular breed. The breeder would need to be satisfied that you had a basic knowledge of the breed's characteristics and what it was originally bred for (*see* pages 19–25.) This should include a discussion of possible breed-related behavior problems. If you are a first-time owner, you will need a great deal of support and advice.

Familiarize yourself with any potential breed-related health problems. For example, short-legged, long-backed Dachshunds may develop spinal and mobility problems.

The breeder will probably ask why you have selected this particular breed and what you want the puppy for—as a pet, for show or for sporting competitions, for example. This may well have a bearing on your choice of puppy, as a puppy with the temperament to be a family pet would not necessarily have—or need—the physical perfection of a show or competition dog. The breeder would need to know about your home and yard and may wish to visit before agreeing to the sale. Most of the questions you are asked are ones you should already have asked yourself (*see* page 14). Once you have purchased the puppy, you should keep in touch with the breeder and share news of the puppy's progress. You will almost certainly need the benefit of further expert advice, and any good breeder would appreciate receiving news about "their" pup.

WATCH OUT FOR UNDESIRABLE PHYSICAL CHARACTERISTICS

Some breed-related characteristics can cause particular health problems of which you should be aware. For example, flat-nosed dogs often have breathing difficulties, short-legged breeds may have movement problems, long-backed dogs can suffer spinal complaints, and breeds with long ears are prone to carrying ticks.

3 Bringing your puppy home

Having chosen your puppy, you and your family will be eagerly awaiting his arrival. However exciting and happy the event may be, this will be a big change—not only for you, but also for your puppy—so take the opportunity to prepare thoroughly. Your puppy is about to be introduced to a whole new world in and around your home, a place full of strange sensory experiences and unfamiliar people, and perhaps other animals, too. This chapter tells you how to ensure that your home is a safe environment, and that you have the necessary equipment for the new addition to the family.

Your puppy and his new home

YOUR PUPPY WILL BE UNSURE AT FIRST, WHICH IS ONLY NATURAL. HE IS COMING TO A STRANGE PLACE WITH UNUSUAL SIGHTS, SOUNDS, AND SMELLS. MOVING INTO A NEW HOME CAN BE STRESSFUL FOR A PERSON AND IT IS JUST AS UNSETTLING FOR A PUPPY, SO MAKE THE ADJUSTMENT AS GENTLE AS POSSIBLE.

A puppy's senses—especially his sense of smell and hearing—are much more acute than ours, so the moment he comes through your door he is being bombarded by odors and noises that will be both confusing and frightening. Try to bear this in mind and take the first few days as quietly as possible. Ask everyone to avoid making too many loud and unexpected sounds that will startle the puppy. This is especially important with regard to young children. Unless he has experience of children from his breeder's home, the puppy will not be used to their excited talking and quick movements and can easily become alarmed.

Once your puppy has started to get used to all the new sensory experiences, you will be able to revert to the hustle and bustle of normal family life without the puppy feeling anxious. It is important that your puppy gets used to all members of the family—both human and animal. Stroke the puppy gently and slowly, and speak soothingly to him to calm him down. Introduce him to every member of the family, but make sure children are supervised by an adult until they learn how to handle the puppy correctly. Let everyone hold and stroke the puppy and talk to him. Knowing he is among friends will go a long way toward putting him at ease.

Encourage any children in the household to help take care of the puppy. Child-friendly chores include feeding the pup, filling his water bowl, and supervised grooming. Encourage your kids to come with you when you exercise the pup, but don't let a child take the leash unless you are sure he or she is old enough to cope and the puppy has learned to walk to heel (*see* page 96) and to return when called (*see* page 90).

Other pets

As soon as possible, let your puppy come into contact with any other pets in the house, such as an older dog, a cat, or a rabbit. At this early age, you may help change your pup's possible preconceived ideas of other animals being either a threat or "prey," so he will grow up thinking of them as friends. Introduce the puppy to the other pet for a brief time, but make sure that you hold both animals fast so there is no chance of injury. Repeat the introductions, steadily increasing the time the animals spend together until both appear to be fully at ease.

How quickly an older dog adjusts to the presence of the newcomer will depend on the character of the adult dog. You should take extra care that a senior dog is not made to feel insecure by the arrival of the puppy. Take special care to ensure that the older dog's "seniority" is respected, not challenged. Always make a fuss of the adult dog and avoid paying too much attention to the puppy while the older dog is around, at least at first. Try not to disrupt the older dog's routine too much. Give the dog his

Let your puppy meet other pets in the house as soon as possible. Gradually lengthen their meetings until the animals become comfortable with each other.

meals at the normal times (always feeding him before the puppy is fed), and exercise him regularly. Make sure he can rest quietly without constantly being pestered by the newcomer.

In the case of a rabbit, let the puppy sniff the hutch and look inside, but don't release the rabbit at first. If the puppy is very excitable, you could remove the rabbit to a safe place and just let the puppy investigate the empty hutch until he is used to it. Then let the puppy see the rabbit inside the hutch for short periods, and reward him when he is calm in the presence of the rabbit. Take care that the rabbit does not become stressed by the sight of the puppy. Once the rabbit is no longer displaying signs of alarm and the puppy is not reacting, introduce them and let the puppy sniff the rabbit, but make sure both animals are held securely.

In the case of cats, try to make sure that neither animal feels intimidated when they meet for the first time. If possible, allow the cat to investigate the newcomer while the puppy is sleeping or in an indoor kennel, pen, or crate. Hold the puppy and slowly introduce him to the

cat, taking care to reassure the pup with gentle stroking and soothing words. Keep the first encounter short, and then slowly increase the time the two animals are together. Soon they'll get accustomed to each other and you should have no problems.

If you have a smaller pet, such as this guinea pig, it will take a while until both animals are perfectly at ease with each other. Give them time to adjust before they meet one-on-one.

Home safety check

BEFORE YOU PICK UP YOUR NEW PUPPY, MAKE SURE YOUR HOUSE AND YARD ARE "PUPPY-SAFE ZONES." BY CHECKING YOUR HOME THOROUGHLY FOR POTENTIAL DANGERS AND THEN DEALING WITH THEM PROMPTLY, YOU CAN PREVENT SERIOUS ACCIDENTS LATER.

In many ways, your puppy is as vulnerable as a human infant—except that he is not only highly inquisitive, but he also moves with surprising speed and has sharp little teeth. For the first few weeks, whenever he is to be left unattended, it is best to confine the puppy to a pen or crate (*see* page 42) in one room. However, it won't be too long before an alert, nosy little puppy will be poking into areas you thought were inaccessible. So it is a good idea to carry out a thorough safety inspection tour before your puppy arrives.

Check the yard

Start your tour of inspection in the yard. Your puppy is still too young to understand that he might be in danger if he runs into the road, so check that there are no gaps in walls and fencing that a puppy could escape through, and make sure that gates can be kept firmly shut. If you have a swimming pool or a deep pond, consider a covering or fencing, since it is only too possible for a pup or an adult dog to drown in a steep-sided pool or pond.

Make sure that all sharp implements are kept shut away. Keep dangerous chemicals, such as pesticides, out of puppy's reach on a shelf, preferably in a lockable hut or garage. Also try to dispose of leftover paints and solvents safely and keep them out of the way, so that your dog will be able to avoid them. Remember, even slug pellets can poison a puppy. Consider switching to safe organic alternatives. Check whether any of your plants may be poisonous. Teething puppies like to chew vegetation, and a surprising number of common plants contain natural toxins that may harm a small dog. They include the common outdoor plants foxglove, ivy, laburnum, lupine, and yew—as well as daffodil bulbs and mistletoe berries—and some indoor plants, such as dumb cane or monstera.

Check the house

There will be times that your puppy is running around freely and your attention is distracted when he may get himself into trouble. You should make thorough safety checks indoors, and encourage all members of the family to be safety-conscious at all times. In particular, make sure everyone understands the need to keep exterior doors shut so that the puppy cannot escape into the road and be injured. If the front door opens onto a busy main road, consider installing a "child gate" or other barrier in the hallway to prevent an escape.

SAFETY TIP

Glass, particularly in patio doors and picture windows, poses a serious hazard as an excitable puppy may not be aware—or may have forgotten—it is there and run straight into it. One solution is to stick brightly colored stickers on the glass at puppy head height, where your pooch can see to avoid it.

Keep household chemicals such as bleach and detergent securely out of reach in cupboards or cabinets. Ensure that you insulate electrical cords or cables with wire guards or covers that the puppy cannot chew through. Never leave small objects lying around that the puppy might swallow. Watch out for sharp objects such as knives or blade edges that the puppy could cut himself on. You should never leave a puppy in the kitchen unattended when food is cooking. As an extra safeguard to avoid scalding, turn the handles of skillets and cooking pots away from the edge of the stove in case the puppy jumps up and knocks one over. (Remember, your puppy may be small now, but large breeds grow quickly, so aim to be safety-conscious from the start.)

Installing a safety gate or barrier can be an effective way to keep your puppy from escaping and getting lost or wandering onto busy streets.

MAKING YOUR HOME PUPPY-SAFE

An exuberant puppy is a little ball of energy. When only a couple of months old, he is surprisingly fast and powerful but lacks the experience to know when his actions may lead him into danger. A few simple precautions can help reduce the risk of harm.

- Keep all pills, especially painkillers, out of reach. Even vitamins and contraceptive pills could be harmful to a puppy.
- Fit a guard over open fires and radiators and all free-standing heaters.
- Take care that hot drinks are placed where a puppy can't knock them over.
- Fit door-slam protectors to keep doors from blowing shut and injuring the puppy.
- Keep all electrical cords and cables out of reach or protect them with chew-proof covers; disconnect electrical appliances when not in use.
- Make sure cords on electric coffee pots and other household appliances are as short as possible, and don't let them hang down where a playful pup can tug at them.
- Don't store leftover paints, solvents, and other chemicals that you have no immediate use for. (It's better to dispose of any residues safely and buy supplies fresh each time, anyway.)
- Make sure children know to put their toys where the puppy can't reach them. Puppies can swallow or choke on small toys and, for reasons of hygiene, infants shouldn't play with toys that puppies have chewed.
- Fit corner pads on any sharp-cornered furniture.
- Low garbage cans can be a danger to your puppy. He'd love to have a curious snoop in the trash if given the chance, but, unfortunately for him, this can lead to a bad case of diarrhea.
- It will take a while for your puppy to get used to climbing and descending stairs, which should remain barricaded until he can use them safely, without tumbling down and possibly injuring himself.

What to buy

YOU'LL NEED CERTAIN BASIC PIECES OF EQUIPMENT BEFORE YOU BRING YOUR NEW PUPPY HOME. ALWAYS BUY GOOD-QUALITY ITEMS FROM WELL-ESTABLISHED RETAILERS. IT COSTS MORE IN THE LONG RUN TO BUY CHEAPER EQUIPMENT THAT DOESN'T LAST AS LONG AND COULD BE DANGEROUS.

The first priority is to select a bed for your puppy to sleep on. There is a wide variety of types to choose from, including dog baskets and dog "nests," or you could use something as simple as a large fluffy blanket folded over several times. Cotton-filled dog beds or duvets are light and colorful. If possible, choose one with a removable cover for washing. If you prefer to use a basket, choose a tough plastic type that will resist chewing. Wicker baskets may look attractive, but they are not very sturdy and if chewed can form dangerous spikes that may injure a puppy. Whichever you choose, to save on cost, make sure that it's big enough to continue to be comfortable for your dog as he grows, especially if you have acquired one of the larger breeds.

Choose a bed that is tough, durable, and easy to keep clean. Avoid beds made of unsafe materials such as wicker, which is easily broken, often producing dangerous spikes.

PUPPY TIP

Try using a large cardboard box lined with blankets to make a good temporary bed for a young puppy during his first days in his new home.

Puppy pen or crate

The largest and most expensive item that you will need for the puppy is his "den," ideally in the form of a sturdy puppy pen or crate. This is where the puppy will sleep and where he will be left when you can't spend time with him. It should be in place before you bring the puppy home so that he associates it with his new home and does not have to become accustomed to it after he has already settled in.

A pen or crate is important, because puppies are vulnerable to injury and should not be allowed to wander around on their own when unattended. They may even find a way out of the house and get lost. When you have other tasks around the house that you have to attend to, you can place the puppy in his crate, safe in the knowledge that he cannot come to harm. In addition, the puppy will feel more secure and gain a stronger sense of "belonging" by knowing he has his own special place. The crate should be big enough to contain his bed, drinking bowl, and a selection of chews and toys to prevent him from getting bored (*see* "Introducing your puppy to his crate"—page 43.) Don't leave your puppy

Consider getting a crate or pen for your puppy. This is the puppy's "home within a home," giving your pet a strong sense of personal security and giving you peace of mind that your puppy is safe when you are not around.

in the crate for long hours during the day. If you must, give him something to play with, and ensure you let him out regularly to relieve himself. Dogs are naturally clean and will not foul their sleeping area, unless they have no other alternative. Your pup may not be fully in control of his eliminations until around six months old, so don't confine him for long periods until he ends up fouling his sleeping area.

GETTING PUPPY USED TO HIS CRATE

Leave the door open initially, so that puppy can wander in and out at will. Play with him, and give him meals and treats in there. If he falls asleep elsewhere, put him in his bed in the crate, so that he will awaken there. This helps him view the bed and crate as his sleeping place. As he gets used to the crate, feed him in there and shut the door. Leave him for a few moments after he has finished eating, and then open the door, so he can come out when he wants. Soon the puppy will see the crate as a good place to be—his little sanctuary. Gradually increase the time that the door is shut when he is inside (two minutes, five minutes, seven minutes, ten minutes) but ensure he has something to do, for example, a chew toy or Kong to play with. If he starts demanding to be let out by barking or whining, don't give in—say nothing, stay out of sight, and wait until he is quiet for at least three seconds, then let him out.

INTRODUCING YOUR PUPPY TO HIS CRATE

Buy a crate that will accommodate your puppy once he is fully grown. Cover three sides with a blanket, so that it resembles a den. Dogs are den-dwelling animals, and this will help to give your puppy a natural feeling of security. Help your puppy to understand that the crate is his place. He should associate it with pleasure, comfort, and security—a place where he can relax and not be disturbed. The crate should not be used as a punishment but should always have positive associations. Try to accustom you puppy to his crate in stages, instead of expecting him to take to it immediately. If your puppy is to sleep in the crate from his first night, you will need to introduce it to him regularly during his first day with you. Put his bed and a couple of safe toys in the crate. Also include a water bowl (buy one with a holder that secures to the side of the crate).

Collar and leash

A simple leather or nylon buckle collar is fine, but make sure you attach an identification tag giving your name and address in case he gets lost. For safety, remove the collar when leaving your puppy unsupervised in his pen/crate. There are a wide variety of leashes available made of

There is a wide variety of colors and styles of collar and leash to choose from. The best are made from hard-wearing leather or nylon mesh.

hemp, leather, or nylon. Plaited or rolled leather styles are more expensive, but also long-lasting and comfortable. Meshed nylon is flexible, durable, and relatively cheap. For your own comfort and your dog's safety, avoid chain collars and leads. Take time in introducing your puppy to his collar. Allow him a few moments to sniff it before you attach it, and choose a time when he is calm and relaxed.

Toys and chews

Your puppy will need a variety of chews in order to exercise his teeth and jaws. Chewing is very important for a puppy to soothe the discomfort of teething. This usually occurs around four to five months, as the "puppy teeth" are replaced, and again around seven months, when the adult

When choosing toys and chews, make sure they can stand up to rough treatment without causing danger to the puppy. Watch out for small, sharp pieces that may break off and get swallowed, and for sharp splinters.

teeth bed down in the jaw. This latter stage can cause intense irritation and may last for several months. If you do not provide suitable items, the pup will find other things to chew, possibly causing serious damage to your home.

There are plenty of edible chews on the market, including rawhide and large marrow bones, and inedible chews such as nylon bones. Offer a selection, as some puppies might prefer something hard to chew while others like soft things to gnaw on. Whatever the puppy chews must be safe and not likely to break into dangerous pieces. Never give cooked bones for this reason. You should also steer clear of small rawhide chews (such as those made in the shape of a slipper), because they can unravel and become stuck in the puppy's throat. They are made to appeal to people rather than dogs.

Safe toys

A wide selection of toys is very important for your puppy's happiness and mental development. Toys can be used as rewards, training aids, to alleviate boredom, stress and anxiety, and, most importantly, as a focus for the interaction between dog and owner. Normal dog behavior, which may be unacceptable in a human environment, can be redirected through the use of toys. It is better to chase a ball or a Frisbee rather than a rabbit, cat, or child. It is preferable to chew a stuffed Kong rather than the furniture or your best shoes. Training problems can often be improved by using a toy. Some puppies are motivated by the prospect of playing with a toy after giving the correct response to a command.

There are many excellent toys on the market, made of safe, natural materials and, of course, owners can always improvise and make their own. A stuffed sock can be an excellent throw toy. Toys should always be chosen with safety in mind. Avoid thin-walled plastic toys, particularly

The prospect of playing with toys, especially as a reward for correctly responding to commands, serves as a great motivation for eager puppies in training.

those containing squeakers, as they can be easily chewed and swallowed. When choosing balls, make sure they are too big to be swallowed. Golf balls can be lethal, as can tennis balls, which puncture easily.

It's important to remember that puppies will not automatically play with their toy when left alone and may need some encouragement. Owners should play with them and motivate and arouse interest. Games should be interactive, challenging, and fun.

Toys and games

If used correctly, toys can keep puppies mentally alert, challenged, and interested in their environment, as well as helping to develop sound relationships with their human family. It is important that owners control the use of toys. They should be kept in a cupboard or box, and the puppy should be given just one or two at a time. Owners should start and finish games and then put the toy away. By doing this, the puppy's interest will be maintained and the owner will be

Use toys during playtime to make games fun and interactive and get everyone involved. It will enhance your puppy's mental and social development.

Balls are good toys for games that involve chasing, but make sure that they are made of safe materials (such as hard rubber and nylon) and the right size for your puppy.

more involved in the play. The owner will also learn which toys the dog finds most rewarding.

Play can be divided into three types of game: chasing, possession, and chewing. Try to select toys that satisfy these instincts.

▌ Games of chase: Balls are an obvious choice for "games of chase," provided that they are a suitable size. Rubber Kongs, which travel in unpredictable directions, are also great fun, as are rubber rings and pull toys, Frisbees, balls on ropes, and rubber rings. One advantage of this type of toy is that the owner must participate and should control the game. The puppy should be taught to sit (*see* page 80) before the toy is thrown, to fetch, and to give it up on command. Some toys designed for chasing games have small ropes attached to their side. The ball is too big to fit in the puppy's mouth, but it can be rolled, chased, and jumped on.

▌ Possession: For games of possession, you can use rubber rings and dog pulls, or rope toys with a ball attached. Tug-type games can be played safely, provided that owners understand that they set the rules and finish the game. Tug games should not involve rough physical play and are unsuitable for young puppies who have not yet learned "bite inhibition" (*see* page 73).

▌ Chewing: For these games, there are cotton rope toys, rubber dental chew toys, stuffed Kongs, cubes, goodie bones, edible rawhide bones, and "nylon bone" dental chews. Puppies can be left alone with them for short periods, but owners should check regularly to make sure these toys remain safe to use.

Toys and games can also be especially useful during puppy training classes, because they can be used as motivation and reward. Having a favorite toy is especially helpful for shy or nervous puppies. This familiar item, linked to home, is very reassuring in an unfamiliar situation. Sometimes a puppy may not respond to a food treat but can be very interested in a toy. In this case, the owner should reward correct responses by playing with the puppy and toy.

Your puppy will enjoy games of chewing and possession. Choose toys for these games that are safe to use.

Handling your puppy

HANDLE YOUR PUPPY OFTEN RIGHT FROM THE START SO THAT HE GETS USED TO BEING TOUCHED BY YOU AND THE REST OF THE FAMILY. GENTLE STROKING IS VERY SOOTHING, AND REGULAR HANDLING WILL MAKE GROOMING EASIER, TOO.

It is important to get your puppy accustomed to being handled all over. It doesn't have to be a chore—done in the right way, it can enhance your bond with him, because handling can be done with great affection. If your puppy is used to being handled, it makes visits to your vet much easier, especially when your puppy needs treatment. It also helps with grooming and assists the staff at boarding kennels. It is not unusual for dogs to be particularly sensitive about having their paws touched, so spend time teaching him to be comfortable with this (see opposite page).

▼ Step 1

Begin by stroking your puppy from head to tail in slow, gentle motions on the side of him that is closest to you. This will help to soothe and calm him.

▼ Step 2

Now pass your hand over his back and onto the side farthest from you and, again, stroke him using long, slow, sweeping movements. Don't rub the puppy briskly, since this can get him overexcited.

HANDLING YOUR PUPPY

When handling your puppy, pay special attention to holding and examining his paws. There may be times when your pup has a thorn or sharp object lodged in his paw that you would have to find and remove, or you may have a puppy whose claws require regular clipping. If he is unaccustomed to having his paws handled, it will make any procedure involving his feet difficult and stressful for both of you. As long as the puppy is relaxed about it, handle all four paws in turn. Spread the toes, and handle the claws—including the dewclaws, if he has any.

If he becomes distressed, talk soothingly to him. (Don't get annoyed or allow the situation to become a battle of wills). Start by just touching the foot and giving a treat (clicking with treating can be useful, too). Using as many treats as you need to, gradually build up the handling until you can do all the steps mentioned previously. Soon, your puppy won't care what you do to his feet, and you can phase out the treats, just giving him warm praise for being such a good little dog.

▼ Step 3

Talk soothingly and give the puppy plenty of treats to gain his confidence as you handle his legs and feet. Slow and gentle stroking will help to calm him down and allow you examine the rest of him.

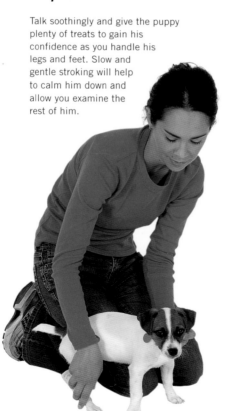

▼ Step 4

Since the tail area is quite vulnerable, most puppies are sensitive about having their tails handled, so take time getting him used to this. It will help you inspect your pup for any health problems.

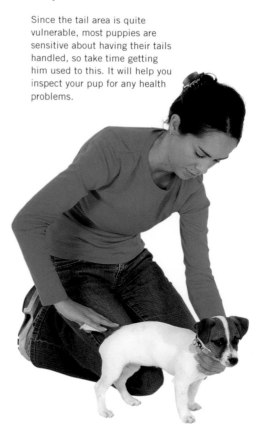

Checking your puppy

JUST AS IT IS IMPORTANT THAT YOUR PUPPY IS USED TO BEING HANDLED, IT IS ALSO NECESSARY FOR YOU TO BE ABLE TO CHECK HIS GENERAL HEALTH. BEING FAMILIAR WITH YOUR DOG'S PHYSICAL CONDITION WILL HELP YOU TO DETECT ANY MEDICAL PROBLEMS AND HAVE THEM TREATED EARLY.

As your puppy gets used to being handled, checking his general health becomes a simple procedure. The following order of inspection will help you get the job done quickly and with little fuss. First handle your puppy gently, so that he feels at ease and secure. Then start by checking his coat, and then his paws, his ears and eyes, his teeth, and finally his tail.

Step 1

Dogs are less likely to resent having their coats touched, because they get used to being stroked. However, this is still a valuable exercise, which, like the others, can be carried out as part of a regular grooming routine. Train your dog to stand still by keeping your hand over his shoulder, holding his collar, or placing a steadying hand on his chest.

Step 2

Although the paws appear quite tough, they can be injured, most notably by grass seeds penetrating between the toes and working into the body through the skin. It is important to check them regularly. Lift the leg, and use one hand to gently spread the toes apart.

CHECKING YOUR PUPPY

Puppies often struggle when having their mouths examined. This is because the mouth and gums can be highly sensitive, particularly as the adult teeth start pushing through at the age of approximately five to six months. At this time, you should check that the milk teeth are dislodging properly. If your puppy is unhappy when you handle his mouth, give him lots of treats and affection to get him used to it. Start by touching the outside of his mouth and give him a treat. Next, gently lift the flap of his mouth, then treat again, and progress to opening his mouth very gently, as the above photos show. Keep treating and reassuring your puppy, and you should be able to examine him easily. Consult your vet if there are any problems.

Step 3

It is not uncommon for dogs to develop ear infections, which can be painful. Any such infection must be treated promptly. Get your puppy used to you checking the outside of the ear flap. Then start lifting the ear. This will make things much easier if, in due course, you need to apply any medication within the ear itself.

Step 4

For cleaning teeth, it is only necessary to slide the toothbrush between the puppy's lips and the outer edge of his teeth. If you need to open your puppy's mouth, use one hand to apply gentle pressure on either side of the mouth, behind the long upper teeth, and with the first two fingers of the other hand, gently pull the lower jaw down.

Step 5

It may seem unnecessary to persuade your dog to allow you to touch his tail, but some dogs can react to being touched here. Just continue stroking him over his tail region at first. Once he is used to this, you can progress to lifting his tail up gently with your hand.

Grooming

GROOMING SHOULD BE A REGULAR PART OF YOUR DOG'S ROUTINE. IT HELPS TO KEEP HIM IN GOOD SHAPE, WHILE YOU STAY IN TOUCH WITH HIS PHYSICAL CONDITION AND GENERAL HEALTH.

Just as it is important for the puppy to get used to being handled from an early age, he should also get used to regular grooming right from the start. Little and often is the secret. Start by using a soft brush and covering only small areas at a time using short, gentle strokes. As you groom, give your puppy plenty of treats and praise, especially whenever he patiently stands

▼ *Step 1*

Your puppy should be in a standing position. Make sure he is relaxed and comfortable—gently place your hand on his chest to steady him. Begin grooming with the rake, using long, even strokes. This prevents matting and is very good for his undercoat.

▼ *Step 2*

A fine-toothed comb is very useful for checking to make sure that your puppy's coat is free of ticks and fleas. Do this by running the comb through his coat, and then holding it up against a light background. Check the comb for any gritty substances, which may be signs of flea dirt.

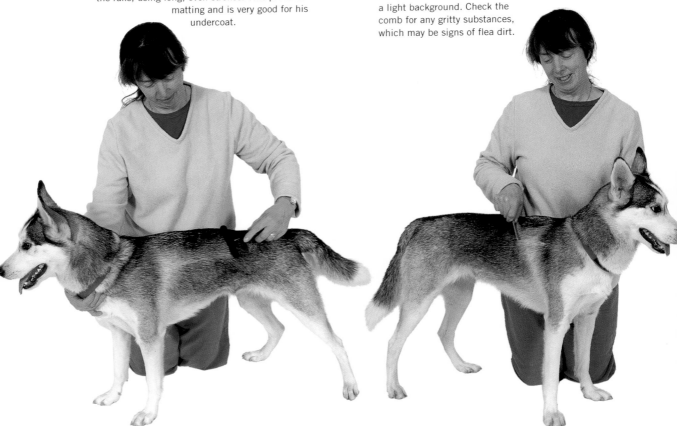

still and lets you groom him. Don't let him play with the brush (or other grooming tools). This can quickly become established behavior that is hard to break, so don't let it start in the first place. If necessary, give him a toy to play with while you groom him.

If you're working on a table, cover it with a mat so the puppy has something for his paws to grip. A shiny, slippery surface makes a puppy feel insecure, and he will be more difficult to groom if he is agitated. For most puppies, a soft brush is sufficient until they are about five months old, when you can start using a rake or comb to remove some of the old, dead hairs and keep the coat from becoming matted. For long-haired breeds, such as the sheltie, you will need to introduce a stiff brush and the comb much earlier than this. Start gently and work on small areas at a time. All breeds need to be groomed regularly, even breeds with smooth, short coats. Long-haired breeds will shed more than smooth-coated breeds.

Give particular attention to the chest, ears, and hindquarters. Once the puppy is used to

Step 3

Next use a brush to condition your puppy's skin and coat. This promotes hair growth by stimulating blood flow to the skin, ensuring that your puppy's coat is full and healthy.

Step 4

Gentle, steady strokes with a grooming glove will remove any remaining old or dead hair, and polish and finish your puppy's coat, leaving it with a healthy shine.

being groomed, you can create a system to keep his coat in good condition, such as:

1. rake (or comb)
2. fine-toothed comb
3. brush
4. grooming glove to finish

If your puppy has long fur, trim the hair around the eyes regularly to ensure good vision and avoid any irritation. Even though your dog may show discomfort, it is very important that you take special care to groom around the anal region. This helps to prevent matting due to fecal buildup, which could cause serious infection.

A rake is ideal for removing dead hair and parasites. It is particularly important for thick-coated and double-coated dogs like retrievers (shown here) as it reaches down to the undercoat.

Dental hygiene

Dental cavities and periodontal gum disease are potentially serious problems with dogs. It is important to start your dental hygiene program as early as possible. Your puppy will first need to get used to the touch of the toothbrush and the taste of toothpaste. (Always use an enzymatic toothpaste specially for dogs, not toothpaste for humans.) Start with a little toothpaste on the brush and gently touch his teeth with it. Once the puppy is relaxed with this, start to brush his teeth, slowly and gently, until the puppy is used to the movement. Use a soft brush and take care to brush the outer surfaces using a gentle circular movement, taking particular care over the gum line where tartar buildup is common.

Avoid brushing too vigorously or you may damage his gums. There is no need to brush the inside surfaces. They are very difficult to reach, and the dog's normal chewing and tongue-rubbing action automatically keeps these surfaces clean.

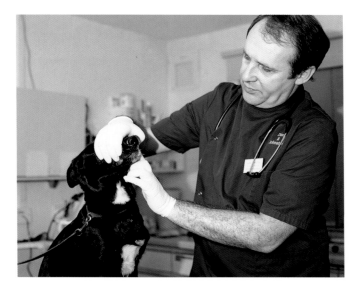

Above Introduce your puppy to toothbrushing as soon as possible. Start slowly, and begin by just touching the teeth lightly with the brush until the puppy is used to the taste and sensation. Then use a gentle, circular motion.

RAW BONES

Some owners give their dogs raw bones to chew to keep their teeth in good condition and reduce the need to brush (as well as providing nutritious marrowbone jelly). Ask your vet to advise you on this. Never give a dog cooked bones to chew, as these easily splinter into sharp pieces that can lodge in his throat or stomach.

Regular examination of your puppy's teeth and gums will alert you to any cavities or infections. Ask your vet for advice on simple and gentle ways to inspect your dog's mouth.

GROOMING EQUIPMENT

1 Rake. This is good for thick-coated and double-coated dogs (such as huskies), since it grooms the undercoat.
2 Metal-toothed "poodle" brush. This is good for curly coats (such as poodles'—hence the name).
3 Grooming glove. One side is covered in brush-like teeth to remove dead hair, the reverse side gives the coat a glossy shine.

(A silk scarf can also be used to polish the coat.)
4 Fine-toothed flea comb. Use this regularly to make sure the coat is parasite-free.
5 Tick remover. As the name suggests, this is used to remove parasites embedded in the skin. Make sure the whole tick is removed, as any part left behind in the skin can cause infection and inflammation.

6 Toothbrush. Choose from a range of soft dental brushes specially designed for puppies.
7 Finger toothbrush. You may find this method easier to follow than using a conventional toothbrush.
8 Enzymatic toothpaste. This helps prevent tartar buildup. It is specially flavored for dogs and is specifically designed to be swallowed (because dogs can't "rinse")!

CLAW TAPPING

Once your puppy is used to having his paws handled (*see* page 49) you can start getting him used to the idea of having his claws clipped. Begin by tapping the claws with the scissors so he is used to the sensation. Then it won't be such a shock when the vet or owner actually clips his claws.

PUPPY GROOMING TIP

If you pick up any grit on a grooming comb, drop it onto a damp paper towel. If it turns red, it is indeed flea dirt and you should consult your vet about this.

Recipes for puppy treats

YOUR PUPPY WILL LOVE THESE TASTY TREATS. IF YOU GIVE SOME AS
REWARD FOR CORRECT BEHAVIOR, THEY WILL PROVIDE THE RIGHT MOTIVATION
TO ENCOURAGE YOUR PUPPY TO PERSEVERE WITH HIS TRAINING.

Garlic-flavored liver treats

Ingredients

1–2 pounds/0.5–1 kilogram liver (calves', pig's
   or lamb's)
garlic granules, powder, or minced garlic
   to your puppy's taste

Method

Place liver in a pan and cover with water. Add
garlic liberally according to your dog's taste, and
bring to the boil. Simmer for 15 to 20 minutes or
until soft. Cut the liver into tiny pieces and place
on foil on a cookie sheet. Bake until hard in a
moderate oven (about 300°F/150°C,) for up to
2 hours, or microwave on full power for about 12
minutes. Cool and then store in an airtight box.

Aunt Liz's liver cake

Ingredients

1 pound/0.5 kilograms liver (calf, pig, or lamb)
1 pound of self-rising flour
1 teaspoon garlic granules or powder
1 medium egg

Method

Liquidize the liver and add the egg and garlic.
Add this mixture to the flour. (Do not put the
flour in the blender or food processor.) Mix well.
Bake in the oven in a large sheet-style cake pan
for approximately 35 minutes at 350°F/180°C.
Store in the refrigerator or cut into individual
portions for freezing. Remove small amounts as
needed and cut into small pieces to give as treats.

Feeding

A GOOD DIET IS VITALLY IMPORTANT FOR A PUPPY. NOT ONLY IS THE RIGHT SELECTION OF NUTRIENTS NECESSARY TO ENSURE THAT THE PUPPY GROWS FIT, STRONG, AND HEALTHY, BUT THE WRONG CHOICE CAN LEAD TO BEHAVIOR PROBLEMS SUCH AS HYPERACTIVITY.

Seek advice on the correct diet for your pet from experts, such as the dog breeder who sold you the dog, an animal nutritionist/dietician, an animal behaviorist (see page 142), or your veterinarian, if he or she specializes in nutrition. Many vets employ a pet nutritionist or could recommend one. (Treat with caution any advice given by specialists who are sponsored by major pet food companies since you can't be sure their advice is impartial.) If you are concerned about possible health or behavioral problems that you think may be diet related, talk to a veterinarian or nutritionist. You may be advised to change the puppy's diet and/or give additional dietary supplements.

A balanced diet

The quantity of food you provide will depend on the age and breed of puppy. The variation can be enormous, from around 250 calories for a three-month-old Yorkshire terrier to nearly 2,000 calories for a Rottweiler of the same age! Serve the food at room temperature, and take care to avoid temperature extremes—neither too hot nor too cold—because your puppy's mouth is highly sensitive. Unlike cats, dogs are not actually true

TEN POSSIBLE DIET-RELATED PROBLEMS

Even though you may provide the best food for your puppy, you will need to feed him the correct amount for optimum health. Too much food will probably result in diarrhea initially. Consistent overfeeding will produce an overweight puppy. Problems such as joint and back disorders, among others, are likely consequences. On the other hand, feeding too little may result in the puppy receiving insufficient nutrients to support his growth, which can cause skeletal problems. A good breeder will provide a diet sheet for your puppy and be eager to offer further advice, if needed. The following health and behavioral problems are sometimes caused by dietary factors such as the wrong balance of ingredients, the presence of certain additives, or a lack of essential nutrients. If you notice these problems with your puppy, seek expert advice and consider changing his diet:

1 Hyperactivity
2 Unexplained restlessness
3 Skin disorders, such as eczema or psoriasis
4 Unexplained redness
5 Skin swellings
6 Soreness/itching
7 Constipation (irregular bowel movements/straining)
8 Diarrhea
9 Dry, peeling, sore nose
10 Dry, sore paw pads

TYPICAL NUTRIENT VALUES OF PUPPY FOOD

The following list is an example of the approximate percentage of ingredients in a typical good-quality "complete" dried puppy food. (Always follow the instructions on the bag when preparing and serving puppy food.)

Protein	25%
Ash	5–6%
Fiber	4–5%
Oil	3–4%
Calcium	1–2%
Phosphorus	1%

Plus vitamins and minerals, including A, D, E, and selenium

carnivores, so they should not be fed an exclusively meat diet. It is essential that your puppy should have a balanced diet containing animal protein and vegetables to ensure that he gets all the vitamins, minerals, proteins, essential fats, and, above all, energy that he needs. One important ingredient is fiber, often neglected in a puppy's diet. But the dog himself often knows instinctively that he must seek out fiber and will chew plants, tree bark, and even wooden furniture in order to make up this deficiency.

It's a good investment to pay a little extra for good-quality, nutritious food for your dog. You can prepare the food yourself using natural ingredients. But if you decide on a manufactured brand, select one that is specially designed for puppies. A rapidly growing

puppy has different dietary needs from those of a full-grown dog. Always check the list of ingredients on labels. Many cheaper brands may lack adequate nutrients and contain extra additives and preservatives that can cause hyperactivity, for example, BHA, BHT, and ethoxyquin. Go for food with natural preservatives like Alpha tocopherol (natural vitamin E). Canned foods may seem like good value for the money, but they have a very high moisture content.

Typically, a well-balanced puppy food will contain meat and bone meal, various cereals such as maize, bran, and oats, rice, animal fats such as chicken fat, oils such as linseed, ash, fiber, and a good range of essential vitamins and minerals.

Your puppy should enjoy a balanced diet that incorporates meat, cereals, animal fats, vegetable oils, vitamins, and minerals.

4 Basic training

Puppies are not naturally willful. Like small children, they need clear and unambiguous guidance from you if they are to figure out exactly what you expect of them. This chapter will explain how to set the rules and the routine for your new puppy's place in the home, and offer guidelines for housetraining, feeding, and grooming. We introduce the clicker and cue words, as well as the techniques for the important first commands that your puppy will learn.

Starting to train your puppy

MAKE SURE YOU GIVE ENOUGH TIME TO ALL ASPECTS OF YOUR PUPPY'S TRAINING. IT IS A PROCESS THAT REQUIRES PATIENCE AND PERSEVERANCE, AND IT IS VITAL TO ESTABLISH AND DEVELOP THE RIGHT RELATIONSHIP WITH YOUR PUPPY. YOU WILL BE REWARDED WITH A HAPPY, OBEDIENT, AND WELL-ADJUSTED DOG.

Just as all children vary in the speed with which they are able to learn new activities, you will find big differences in how quickly different puppies manage to learn correct behavior. Some puppies are very quick to understand what it is you want them to do, while others need much more time and patience. Nevertheless, all puppies are eager to please and enjoy warm praise, attention, and treats, so you can be sure they will be only too ready to do whatever they can to earn your approval.

Training with treats and praise will play on your puppy's natural curiosity and his eagerness to make him want to earn your approval.

If you are willing to spend some time each day training your puppy—even if you can only spare five minutes—you will soon find that your puppy rewards your patience and attention by learning forms of behavior that ensure that he is a credit to you and a joy to have around.

Setting the rules

If possible, arrange some vacation time when you first acquire the puppy so he has plenty of time to get to know his surroundings and to settle into a routine. The whole family can then be involved in his basic training—especially housetraining—before the puppy has to be left for the first time. It is important that all members of the family know the "house rules" as they apply to the puppy. These must be agreed upon and applied consistently by everyone from the moment the puppy arrives home. Will he be allowed on the furniture? What about upstairs? Are any areas of the house off-limits? The family must decide the

WARNING! HANDS OFF

Any form of physical violence directed against a puppy is not only cruel and cowardly but totally pointless, more likely to enforce bad behavior than correct it. Ill-treatment may trigger a dog's "passive defense reflex," leading to a painfully timid animal, or alternatively activate his "active defense reflex," producing a hostile and potentially dangerous animal.

rules and stick to them or you will have a very confused puppy.

Speaking the language

It is very important that you understand that puppies do not understand English (or any other human language). This probably seems obvious, yet many owners still act as if they believe that so long as they shout or talk slowly and succinctly in sentences, the puppy will somehow know what he should—or should not—do. Puppies can, in time, learn simple cue words such as "sit" and "stay." They are unlikely to understand whole phrases such as "stop doing that," "get off that chair," and "you are a bad dog," although they will understand tone of voice. Even more important, they are unlikely to see a connection between your cross words and angry face and any action of theirs that may have displeased you, if the "bad deed" took place minutes before.

Both puppies and adult dogs have an associative memory of about three seconds, so it is pointless to scold them for something done minutes or hours before. It is far better to reward a puppy when he does something right, than punish him when he does something wrong. If a puppy does not understand why he is being scolded, he will simply assume that irrational outbursts are a normal aspect of your behavior and he will eventually stop trying to please. For this reason, rather praise and reward good behavior.

Types of treats

Make sure your puppy knows when he is performing correctly by immediately rewarding good behavior with treats and praise. There are many types of treats that you can offer. On page 56, we give recipes for hard-baked garlic-flavored liver treats that most puppies really love. Put some in a small jar or plastic container that you can keep with you at all times, perhaps tucked inside a pocket or bag. Cheese is another favorite with puppies. Sometimes it's a good idea to let the puppy see and sniff the treat so he knows that a reward is coming. You can also "treat" a puppy by letting him play with a favorite toy (*see* page 47). The most important treat of all is to praise the puppy when he performs really well. Gently stroke him, and say his name along with warm, soothing talk. The tone of voice is more important than the words themselves. With these techniques, he will be eager to practice his new obedience skills in order to earn your approval again. Be aware that it is not a good idea to pet your puppy with a brisk rubbing action because he can get overexcited when handled in this way. A calm voice and gentle stroking will make sure that you are a secure and reassuring presence in your puppy's world.

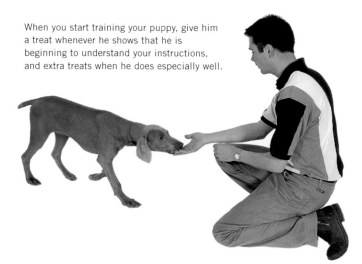

When you start training your puppy, give him a treat whenever he shows that he is beginning to understand your instructions, and extra treats when he does especially well.

Clicker training

THE HIGHLY SUCCESSFUL, REWARDS-BASED STYLE OF TRAINING USED IN THIS BOOK INVOLVES A TECHNIQUE CALLED "CLICKER TRAINING," SO-CALLED BECAUSE IT EMPLOYS A SMALL, SIMPLE TEACHING AID CALLED A CLICKER.

This hand-held device does exactly what you would expect—it clicks. This click is a signal that tells your puppy: "Yes! That's right! Well done! A reward is coming!" This is known as "click-and-treat"—a click followed by a food tidbit or other treat—and this phrase will appear in many of the step-by-step instructions given in this book, especially for basic training. The clicker acts as a marker to indicate correct behavior. The clicker is not used as a command. Nor should it be used to gain your puppy's attention.

Before commencing your training, you slowly "tune in" your puppy to the sound of the clicker. Start by simply clicking and giving him a treat several times over—without expecting him to do anything in return. Don't click in your puppy's face, but muffle the sound initially—by clicking in your pocket—until he gets used to the sound

and associates it with something pleasant, like a treat. Watch for any movement or sign that indicates the puppy is beginning to associate the sound of the clicker with a food treat. Very soon the clicker itself becomes the main indicator that he has performed correctly.

Advantages of clicker training

Clicker training is a more accurate communicator than praise. It helps your puppy to concentrate, because it removes the need for him to try to pick out the one word that he may understand from all the words and sounds he may be hearing. Also, the clicker easily transfers from person to person—the click sounds the same whoever does it. It is completely positive and it is never emotional—you can't make a clicker sound cross or upset. The clicker can also be used over distances.

Remember that while teaching your puppy using this method, there is no place for any form of punishment (not even "No!"). If your puppy gets it right, he gets a reward. If he gets it wrong, there is no reward. Once "tuned" to the clicker, the sight of it is enough for most dogs to respond enthusiastically. You can start each session with a couple of free click-and-treats if you like to make sure he knows "the game is afoot."

The basics of clicker training

Start each session with a hungry puppy and stop while he is still eager and interested. Keep at it!

The clicker is a useful aid to training. It tells your puppy clearly and unambiguously when he has performed well and can expect a reward.

Practice regularly but for very short periods only. Short regular practice sessions are the most effective. Just like a human, a puppy learns best when he is mentally alert, and his attention will wander when he gets mentally and physically fatigued, so limit the sessions to no more than five minutes at a time.

At first, work on one obedience skill at a time. Take a break or change to another area or part of the room before beginning to work on another command. When teaching a new command, always click-and-treat every time at first. Then "tease" to see if he is getting the idea. Click-and-treat a correct response. Relax and be patient—there is no need to rush. If using a lure, such as a treat in your hand to lure the puppy into position, try to phase out the lure as soon as possible by pretending to have a treat in your hand. Eventually, your hand movement alone will have become a signal to your puppy. Then click the correct response, and treat from your pocket. Use this as often as possible. You could also try to introduce alternative reinforcements, such as praise, a game, a walk, or whatever.

Time your click!

The clicker is used to indicate "Great job! That is the response I wanted," so you must always time the click so that your puppy hears it when he is responding correctly. The click must be immediate. For example, click when you have asked the puppy to "sit" and he is actually sitting down—it is no use clicking a "sit" after he has stood up again!

Reinforcing and motivating

It is important for your puppy to receive frequent reinforcement in the early stages so that he remains highly motivated to keep trying. When you are working on a "down," for example, you don't need to wait for the puppy to go right down

"Tune in" your puppy to the clicker device by clicking and giving him a food treat several times, so that he starts to associate the sound with a reward.

perfectly before you reinforce his actions with a click-and-treat. Watch out for any movement that looks likely to lead to your end goal, and click-and-treat that. Then, by small steps, you will progress toward the desired behavior.

When he has achieved the complete movement, give him a jackpot—click, lots of treats, and warm praise. Get into the habit of giving your puppy extras for excellence. Let him know that you are delighted with him. It will motivate him, and he'll work even harder. Over the weeks, gradually aim to increase his motivation still further by trying to get two or three correct responses for one click-and-treat, and then progress to click-and-treat at random.

CLICKER DOS AND DON'TS

✔ Do click when the puppy has performed well.
✔ Do time your click so that the puppy hears it while he is behaving correctly.
✔ Do keep the clicker in your pocket or behind your back at first (since puppies are sensitive to sound).
✘ Don't click to attract your puppy's attention.
✘ Don't click in front of your puppy's face.
✘ Don't click incorrect behavior.

Cue words

CUE WORDS ARE VERBAL INSTRUCTIONS THAT ENABLE YOUR PUPPY TO IDENTIFY WHAT ACTION YOU WOULD LIKE—FOR EXAMPLE, "SIT," "LEAVE IT," OR "DOWN"—ONCE YOU HAVE TAUGHT HIM THE CORRECT CUE-COMMAND ASSOCIATION.

Cue words shouldn't be introduced immediately. Your puppy first has to respond correctly or he won't be able to associate the command with the action. Initially, your puppy is simply following the food lure, but with practice, he will start to link the hand movement with the action. When he is at this stage, you can start teaching the command without holding the treat, but moving your hand in the same way as you did when you held the treat (this has become a hand signal).

Once the response is 99 percent predictable, you can add the cue word—the command or name of the response, such as "sit," "down," or "stand." However, using the cue word before the response is established just teaches your puppy that the cue is meaningless. Never use cue words until you are virtually certain you can get the required response. Then the order is cue word with hand signal/response/click-and-treat.

The whole family must be absolutely consistent in the use of cue words. One way to achieve this is to draw up a puppy dictionary sheet and make sure everyone keeps it updated and refers to it constantly. It doesn't actually matter what cue word you use. You could say "sausage" instead of "sit" and "doughnut" for "down," and the puppy would still respond correctly—just so long as the same word is used by everyone involved.

Make sure your cue word is clear but quiet, especially if your puppy is beside you (a dog's hearing is very acute), and that it sounds the same each time it is used. Never use the cue word in anger. Once you have your puppy's attention, use the cue word once—and once only. If he doesn't respond, it is probably because he does not yet understand the cue word. Repeating the cue word and—worse still—saying it over and over in ever-increasing volume ensures that your puppy only responds to the tenth command shouted loudly!

It may take 60 to 100 tries before your puppy reliably associates the cue with the response. Once a response is learned and on cue—that is, your puppy is responding to a command—it is important that you no longer reinforce random performances of that action (such as sitting), but only reinforce it when you have asked for it.

Play games with your puppy, so he has to wait for the cue to be given before the response is reinforced. The aim is for the puppy to respond appropriately to a cue, so this is an important part of the learning process. It is well worth spending some time on this.

MAKE LEARNING FUN!

Training sessions should be fun for both you and your puppy. Keep sessions brief—just a few minutes several times a day. Play lots of games with your puppy and make sure he has enough suitable, safe toys (such as Kongs, rope toys, and rubber balls or nylon bones) to indulge his natural instinct for chasing, possessing, and chewing (see page 44.) Let him play with just one or two toys at a time. Make sure you're the one who always initiates and finishes any games.

Vary the surroundings

Teach the command again in a variety of places and circumstances—at least eight to ten. But be prepared to lower your standards when you teach in a new place. Puppies take in everything about their surroundings. They often understand and respond correctly in one place, but if asked for that behavior somewhere else (or if you are sitting when you normally stand), they get confused and do not know what is expected of them. Once your puppy is used to performing the "sit," for example, in eight to ten different locations, he will have made the connection and will understand that "sit" means "sit" wherever he is and whatever he is doing.

Herding dogs, such as this border collie, are able to learn and practice their skills through the use of cue words, whistles, and hand signals.

Housetraining

HOUSETRAINING (FORMERLY CALLED "HOUSEBREAKING") IS A
JUDICIOUS MIXTURE OF DOG KNOWLEDGE, OBSERVATION, AND
COMMON SENSE. GIVEN THE RIGHT OPPORTUNITIES, PUPPIES
HAVE NO DESIRE TO FOUL THEIR LIVING OR SLEEPING QUARTERS.
IF OWNERS USE THIS KNOWLEDGE, THEY CAN SOON TEACH THEIR
PET THE APPROPRIATE PLACES TO USE.

Female dogs keep their puppies and the whelping nest scrupulously clean. Puppies instinctively move out of the nesting area to eliminate as soon as they are mobile enough to do so. But this early training by the mother is often nullified by human error, when puppies are left for too long a period without the opportunity to get to a suitable spot and are forced to use what seems to them to be the most appropriate place at a time of urgent need. Perseverance, patience, and perhaps being tolerant of a little inconvenience during this tricky time can pay dividends later on.

Whatever you do, try not to overreact if your puppy soils indoors. An extreme response to "accidents" at this time can often cause irreparable harm to the owner/pet relationship before it has even become properly established. Punishing a dog for house soiling is pointless. After all, the puppy is doing something natural and necessary, just not in the appropriate place. Any correction given more than three seconds after the act will not be associated with the incident and will confuse the puppy.

In fact, any exaggerated reaction to accidental soiling can lead to problem behavior. Rather than understanding that you are only opposed to soiling in the house, your puppy might think you are against urinating and defecating anywhere, and may become reluctant to "go" when you are around. A confused and anxious puppy is more likely to eliminate in the wrong place, or he may only try to "go" when you are away, or to find a "secret" place that he can use, so the house-soiling problem will only be exacerbated.

If you catch the puppy in the act, simply pick him up, hustle him outside while saying "outside, outside...," and then praise him if he continues to go in the yard. At all other times grit your teeth, ignore the accident, and be nice to your puppy as he rushes up to greet you.

Communicate with your pup

Puppies learn much more quickly when they are rewarded for doing the right thing than if they are punished for making a mistake. Sometimes we fail to communicate to the puppy the one vital factor that will make all the difference: "Don't do it here, do it out there!" Owners who have at first used newspaper to train their puppy often have this problem when they try to persuade the puppy to abandon the paper and use the yard instead: The puppy does not understand the significance of newspaper, but he will think you are encouraging him to use that area of floor.

Once the puppy gets used to using that area, he will become confused when you want him to start going outside. At first you were praising the puppy for relieving himself on the paper in the kitchen; now you are punishing the puppy for doing the same thing when you have removed the paper. "First I was praised for going indoors, now it is wrong to go indoors. Why can't they make up their minds?" It can take time for the puppy to understand exactly what is required of him and reward-based training is the only way to success.

The science of animal behavior also reveals that urinating and defecating are scent-related activities, and that dogs will be drawn back to the same spot that they used previously, if even a vestige of smell remains. The dog's nose being far superior to ours means that even when we clean the area to our satisfaction, he may still be able to detect a faint remaining odor. It is advisable to use odor-eliminating products available from your vet or pet store and to follow instructions carefully.

Bathroom breaks

Common sense tells us that it is likely that your puppy will need to relieve himself at certain times. At first he needs to be taken outside every hour to one-and-a-half hours. Later on, the most likely times are when he has just woken up, after vigorous activity and after feeding. It makes sense to watch for these occasions and to make certain that you take the puppy outside to the spot that you want him to use for this purpose. Use a word of encouragement that the puppy can associate with the activity, and then praise him when he performs in the correct place.

Other signs that will tell you that your puppy needs to "go" include urgent sniffing of the floor, looking for a suitable place to relieve himself, and running to the door (a good sign that indicates that your puppy is getting the

Watch for signs that your puppy needs to relieve himself, and then take him outside to the place that you want him to use as his "bathroom."

message). Be particularly suspicious if your puppy is sniffing an area that he has soiled previously, and get him outside immediately.

The quickest way to help a puppy to become clean overnight is to use a puppy pen or crate (*see* page 42.) This restricts the pup to an area close to his sleeping place and encourages him to hold on until you can let him out. It is essential that the puppy goes straight from the crate to the yard in these circumstances. It is also an advantage to have the crate in a place where you can hear if the puppy becomes restless during the night so that you can get up and let him out then. The fewer mistakes the puppy makes, the sooner you will be successful. A few disturbed nights are a small price to pay for this.

Keep the nights as short as possible. Take your puppy outside as late in the evening as you can and again first thing the next morning. If the puppy has to be left alone for any time during the day, try to arrange for a neighbor or friend to call and let the puppy out so that he can stick to the routine he is developing.

That "guilty" look

Do not be deceived into thinking that because your puppy "looks guilty" he knows what he has done wrong. Your puppy is simply reacting to your facial expression, body posture, and tone of voice. He will certainly know that you are angry, but he will not associate your anger with having soiled the carpet half an hour ago. If he does make a connection, it will be the presence of the feces and his owner in the same room that causes the puppy's unhappiness—not the act of soiling. Always reward the puppy for getting it right. Don't punish him for getting it wrong.

Try to learn the signs that indicate that your puppy has an urgent need to urinate or defecate and get him outside as soon as possible.

(see page 42.)

DIET AND HOUSETRAINING

Your puppy's diet could influence housetraining. Dogs differ as to what foods suit them—some are allergic to certain foods, such as wheat. If you feed cheap brands of kibble, your puppy may eat more to obtain all the nutrients he needs, resulting in large volumes of loose stool. Other problems affect housetraining, too. For example, being unable to "hold it" overnight could be because your dog's feeding time makes it necessary for him to relieve himself just before you usually get up. You might try out different feeding times, but remember that your pup might not have complete control over his bodily functions until he is at least six months old, so don't be harsh with him.

Don't scold your puppy for any "accidents" he has indoors, but clean the area with a strong non-ammonia-based disinfectant or an odor-eliminating product so he is not encouraged by the smell to use that area again.

Once your puppy has performed successfully outside, make a big fuss over him and give him treats so he understands that you are very pleased with him.

Reward your puppy with treats and praise once he performs successfully outside. This tells him that he has done the right thing.

Problem behavior

THE MOST COMMON PROBLEM BEHAVIORS AMONG PUPPIES INCLUDE JUMPING UP ON PEOPLE, BEGGING FOR FOOD, AND PROBLEM BARKING. NEVER ENCOURAGE ANY BAD BEHAVIOR OR THE PUPPY WILL THINK THAT IT IS PERFECTLY ACCEPTABLE.

Jumping up

There is a reason why pups jump up. It is a greeting behavior that they have learned brings them attention. By touching the puppy, even if only to push him down, and talking to him, saying—for example—"no," "stop that," or "get down," you are rewarding the puppy for jumping up by giving him the attention he craves. Instead, you must ignore the puppy. Look down and away from the puppy so you don't catch his eye. If necessary, turn your body away, if you're sitting down, or stand up and turn your back on the puppy. Continue until the puppy stops jumping up. Gently and quietly praise him when he has all four feet on the ground. Once he realizes that he is not going to get your attention or praise by jumping up, he will stop doing it.

Above Discourage jumping up by ignoring the puppy when he does it; any verbal or physical responses from you will give him the attention he desires.

Jumping up: Step 1

Averting your gaze and turning away every time will teach your puppy that there is no reward for jumping up and that he will earn your approval only once he has all four feet on the ground.

Step 2

Systematically ignoring your puppy's jumping will yield gradual results, not instant solutions. Make sure that you treat your puppy and give him lots of praise and attention when he stops jumping up and is standing on all fours.

Begging

The same principle applies to begging. Once your puppy knows that you will share your food with him if he sits patiently gazing up at you appealingly, he will continue to do it. It may seem hard-hearted, but you must ignore the puppy whenever he begs until he accepts that you are not going to weaken. You must also be very firm on this point with other family members, visitors to your home, and with other people that you meet out of doors. Otherwise, even if your puppy leaves you alone, he will consider all strangers as "easy targets" and beg for scraps whenever he sees someone eating.

Problem behavior should never be encouraged or your puppy will think that it is perfectly acceptable.

Barking

Guard dog breeds have been specially selected to bark when there are strangers around, and this may be one of the reasons you acquired a dog in the first place. However, problem barking may occur mainly because the dog is overexcited or frightened, most commonly because he is being left alone for long periods and he's bored. Ask a friend or neighbor to look after your puppy when possible, or swing by the house from time to time to reassure your pup. Also leave safe toys with him, so he has something to do when on his own.

When you are eating, ignore any plaintive appeals for food—your puppy should be given food only when *you* decide, so never encourage begging for scraps.

Bite inhibition

A PUPPY'S BITE CAN BE PAINFUL, BUT HIS TEETH AND JAWS ARE NOT POWERFUL ENOUGH TO CAUSE SERIOUS DAMAGE. HOWEVER, PUPPIES SHOULD BE TAUGHT HOW TO CONTROL THEIR BITING INSTINCT WHILE THEY ARE STILL YOUNG. OTHERWISE, WHEN THEY ARE OLDER, THEY CAN BE A DANGER TO OTHER ANIMALS, TO PEOPLE AND, ULTIMATELY, TO THEMSELVES.

As you may soon discover, your puppy has small, sharp, needle-like teeth—and they're there for a very good reason. It's not to chew the curtains or your best shoes, but to teach your puppy how to control his bite. When a puppy is suckling and

chomps a bit too hard on the nipple, his mother will react. She will make a growling sound and may get up, shake herself, and walk away. When a puppy is playing with his brothers and sisters in the litter and bites one of them hard enough

Through play and interaction with each other, puppies learn about "bite inhibition"—how to use their teeth and jaws appropriately.

to cause pain, the injured party yelps and may retaliate or spring away.

From this, the puppy learns that when he bites it hurts. He also learns that when he does this, he no longer gets fed and playtime stops, and so he starts biting less and less. He is learning something called "bite inhibition"—that is, understanding when it is inappropriate to use his teeth and jaws.

Puppies are often taken away from their mother and the rest of the litter before they have fully mastered bite inhibition (*see* page 19.) So their owners must take over the task and include it in the puppy's training program. In a multidog household, other dogs will help to teach a young puppy bite inhibition through natural interaction and play, but you should still check to make sure that it is being correctly learned.

It is absolutely vital that puppies master bite inhibition before they are four or five months old. After this time, they start to lose their first set of delicate "puppy teeth," and their large, sturdy adult teeth begin to come through. Their jaws become more powerful and, if they are still biting, they enter a difficult stage. If a juvenile or adult dog has not mastered bite inhibition, he may get overexcited and bite another animal (or worse) a child, too hard, causing injury. The fact that the dog may not have intended to bite so hard will not be accepted as a valid excuse by the injured parties and their parents or owners.

Teaching bite inhibition

Bite inhibition must be taught by the adult owners of the puppy. Simply offer the puppy your fist and let him mouth and nibble your hand. When the bite becomes hard enough to reach your pain threshold, keep your hand totally still— that is important—but react firmly with a sharp

"ouch!" or "aargh!," as you would if you were the puppy's mom. Don't pull your hand away or the puppy will think it's a game and continue to bite. The reaction should cause the puppy to withdraw from your hand. When he does, change your tone of voice entirely. Praise him—"What a good puppy!"—click your clicker, if you've got it handy, give him a treat, and stroke him.

If, however, your puppy doesn't stop mouthing when you say "ouch!," imitate the mother and say nothing, get up, ignore him for approximately thirty seconds, and then go back and do the whole thing over again. Using the "ouch!" method does not mean your pup will never mouth you again simply because you've said "ouch!" but it does mean that gradually his biting will occur less and become softer.

You must do this exercise regularly, several times a day. Gradually, over the next few weeks, you should say your "ouch!" earlier and earlier in the pain threshold until there is no mouthing at all. You should reach the point where you say "ouch!" if the puppy puts his mouth anywhere near your hand—even if it doesn't hurt. Never allow your puppy to mouth shoelaces, clothing, or any part of the body other than the hands.

STAGES OF LEARNING BITE INHIBITION

Stage 1: Offer your puppy your hand to mouth. Say "ouch!" when he bites too hard.

Stage 2: Let your puppy mouth your hand, but say "ouch!" to soften the bites gradually.

Stage 3: Puppy's bite inhibition should be improving well. Say "ouch!" for any contact between his teeth and your hands.

Stage 4: By now, your puppy should not be mouthing you at all.

Bite inhibition: Step 1

Offer your hand to the puppy, and then give a stern and abrupt "ouch!" reaction when his bites grow too harsh. This is his signal for knowing when to stop, because to him your reaction will be one of disapproval. He will learn to remove his mouth from your hand. When he does so, remember to click, and reward him with warm praise, affection, and lots of treats.

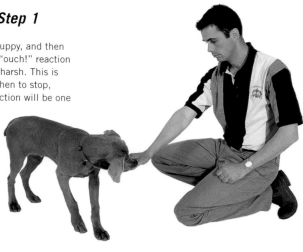

Step 2

If your pup does not respond to the "ouch!" reaction, then walk away and ignore him for a few minutes. This emulates the type of response the puppy would have had from his mother, which to him means less food and less play. Eager to keep your approval, he will gradually learn to refrain from mouthing altogether. You must practice this exercise several times a day to get the best results.

Step 3

Regular practice should have the eventual result of no mouthing at all, especially if "ouch!" is uttered at gradually earlier instants during the biting process. Always reward your puppy with lots of praise and treats, so that he knows he has given the correct response.

Getting attention

IT IS VITAL FOR YOUR RELATIONSHIP WITH YOUR PUPPY THAT HE IS ABLE
TO LEARN FROM YOU, ESPECIALLY WHEN TRAINING HIM IN OBEDIENCE.
HE NEEDS TO KNOW YOU ARE THE LEADER, AND THIS IS WHY GETTING
HIS ATTENTION IS CRUCIAL.

Being able to hold your puppy's attention is an essential part of his training that will greatly assist you when teaching him commands, such as "sit," "stand," or "down." The technique for this is known as "watch me," and it entails getting your puppy to fix his attention on you through the use of the clicker and treats. "Watch me" is also a highly effective way of gaining your puppy's attention when he is distracted and calming him down when he is excited. It helps to enhance your control and you can use it as a preliminary instruction to get your puppy to look at you before asking him to carry out a command. The treats encourage your puppy to realize the benefits of focusing on you. This technique is worth extensive practice—the better you are able to hold your puppy's attention, the greater the progress the two of you will make.

Left Practice getting your puppy's attention. Use the "watch me" technique demonstrated on pages 78 and 79.

Right Being able to get his attention is an essential part of teaching your puppy the important commands that form part of his training.

Watch me

"WATCH ME" IS A TECHNIQUE THAT INVOLVES TRAINING YOUR PUPPY TO LOOK AT YOU FOR GRADUALLY INCREASING PERIODS OF TIME. IT IS A VALUABLE COMMAND TO TEACH A PUP. ONCE HE LEARNS IT, IT WILL ENABLE YOU TO EXERCISE A GREAT DEGREE OF CONTROL OVER HIM.

"Watch me" is taught in stages: Get your puppy to look at you, then click-and-treat. Gradually increase to five seconds, ten, and then fifteen, until you can hold his attention for twenty seconds. This requires frequent practice, not just at home, but in many different places, such as the yard, the park, and when visiting friends. Once your puppy is doing this correctly on a regular basis, change your approach by keeping the treat in your pocket or bag. Hold your hand to the puppy's nose, then up to your face and when he is watching you, click and give him the treat.

▼ Step 1

Show your puppy a food treat in your hand, and then raise it to your face. Click-and-treat when the puppy looks at you. Gradually increase this time to five seconds.

▼ Step 2

Now, with food in your hand, try to build up keeping your puppy's attention on your face for between ten and fifteen seconds. If he looks away, put the food on his nose and start again. Start using the cue words "watch me" while he is looking at you. Click-and-treat and praise.

WATCH ME

When teaching your puppy the "watch me" technique, remember that the most important point about this exercise is being able to gain and hold his attention. It is not so much about achieving a specific posture or getting him to concentrate while maintaining a certain position, such as "sit" or "stand." (Although when learning "watch me," your puppy would be naturally inclined to sit, since his rear will go down as his nose goes up to follow the lure of the treat!). The aim of "watch me" is to get your puppy to understand that he should focus his attention on you. This is a very important exercise as once he has mastered this, you will be able to get his attention in any situation or position, for instance, when you are out walking and surrounded by numerous distractions like other people and their dogs.

▼ Step 3

Without holding a food treat, use your hand as a signal. Click when he is looking at you and then give him the reward from your pocket.

▼ Step 4

Gradually you will phase out the hand signal, and simply use the cue words. Remember to praise your puppy and give him lots of attention for doing it right!

 # Sit

AVOID CUE WORDS WHEN YOU FIRST TEACH YOUR PUPPY SOMETHING NEW, IN THIS CASE THE COMMAND FOR "SIT." INSTEAD, CLICK AND TREAT AS SOON AS HE RESPONDS. PRACTICE THIS SEVERAL TIMES A DAY, AND TRY INTEGRATING IT INTO YOUR DOMESTIC ROUTINE. FOR EXAMPLE, GET THE PUPPY TO SIT BEFORE HE HAS HIS BREAKFAST.

When teaching your puppy to "sit," place the treat close to his nose, without touching it. Then slowly raise your hand back over the puppy's head, so that his nose rises up to follow the treat. As this happens, his rear will descend, and the puppy should then sit automatically. Initially, reward every correct response with a click-and-treat and warm praise, so that he knows he has done what you wanted.

 ### Step 1

With the puppy in a standing position, bring the treat close to his nose so he can smell that you are holding something tasty.

Step 2

Lift your hand backward over the puppy's head, so that his nose follows the treat and his rear begins to lower during the movement.

SIT

When teaching "sit," be careful not to lift your hand too high over the puppy's head, otherwise he will be encouraged to jump up or stand, and this will confuse him, too. Introduce the cue word only once you are satisfied that your puppy is reliably sitting in response to the lure, when you can begin to say it as he is going into the position. Phase out using treats in your hand as soon as possible. Use your hand as a signal, and treat from your pocket. Once the pup is sitting reliably, give rewards on a random basis: treat one "sit," two "sits," then three, and so on, so he never knows when a reward is coming.

▼ Step 3

The process has brought the puppy into a natural "sit" position.

▼ Step 4

Once you have the correct response, use the clicker immediately so the puppy knows he has done the right thing.

▼ Step 5

Give your puppy the treat and lots of praise for getting it right.

Down

TEACHING YOUR PUPPY TO LIE DOWN ON CUE IS A USEFUL CONTROL EXERCISE, ESPECIALLY AT TIMES WHEN YOUR PUP IS OVERLY EXCITED OR WHEN THERE ARE OTHER PEOPLE AND/OR ANIMALS AROUND.

Take the time to teach your puppy as many cue words or commands as possible. Not only will this make him easier to handle, it will also help to encourage brain activity and coordination.

Regular practice ensures a positive relationship between you and your puppy. Gradually he will learn to trust and obey you, while you enjoy the pleasure of a happy and obedient pet.

Step 1

Show your puppy a food treat in your hand. Make sure he understands that you are holding something yummy that he likes.

Step 2

Holding on to the treat, run your hand down your puppy's chest, between his two front legs, and onto the floor.

DOWN

Start teaching your puppy commands as early as possible. Not only will this foster a stronger bond between you, but it will also stimulate better responses from your puppy because he is being encouraged to think and learn. It is very important that you use treats to lure your pup into performing commands; do not actually push him into any position. In physical terms, puppies need to learn and assume bodily postures of their own accord in order to acquire the necessary "muscle memory" that enables them to recall and carry out the actions that make up a position. "Down" is an exercise that needs a fair amount of muscle memory because it employs several different types of muscular activity at the same time. Puppies flop down quite easily, but when older dogs lie down, you can see that it takes a lot more effort than when they were younger.

▼ *Step 3*

Holding the treat under your hand, keep your hand still and wait. Normally, the pup will try to get the treat out from under your hand and, in doing so, will lie down.

▼ *Step 4*

Give your puppy lots of affection and praise for doing well.

Stand

GETTING YOUR PUPPY TO STAND ON COMMAND CAN BE VERY USEFUL, PARTICULARLY FOR TRICKY SITUATIONS WHEN MOST DOGS STRUGGLE TO KEEP STILL AND RELAXED: GROOMING, DOG SHOWS, AND VISITS TO THE VET!

Teach your puppy "stand" by starting with a "sit" position. Show him a treat, and then lower your hand a little below his nose—not too low or he will end up lying down. Bring your hand forward, and as the puppy's nose follows the treat, he will go into a "stand." Click right away, but keep your hand that is holding the treat still, otherwise the puppy will start walking in pursuit of the food. Then give him the treat and lots of praise for a successful "stand."

▼ Step 1

Start with your puppy in a "sit" position and show him a treat.

▼ Step 2

Carefully drop your hand until just below the puppy's nose. If you lower your hand too far, the puppy may mistake your hand movement for your "down" signal and lie down.

STAND

Since you started by training your pup to sit, this behavior will be strongly conditioned in him. When teaching "stand," it is not unusual for the puppy to stand when you bring your hand forward, but then automatically resume the "sit." Be sure that you are completely aware of what the puppy is doing, so that as he stands, you click immediately before he sits again. Continue doing this, and eventually your puppy will discover the connection between the click and the position you are asking of him. Once he finds the "right place" for the click, he will know what to do.

Step 3

Bring your hand forward very slightly—not too far or the puppy will start to walk. Your hand movement serves merely as a passive guide into the "stand" position. As soon as he is standing, click to confirm that he has done what you wanted.

Step 4

Remember to reward your puppy's correct responses with treats and praise.

Recall

"RECALL" INVOLVES TRAINING YOUR PUPPY TO COME TO YOU. IT IS IMPORTANT TO START TEACHING THIS TECHNIQUE AS EARLY AS POSSIBLE SO THAT YOUR PUPPY WILL LEARN FROM THE START TO COME TO YOU WHEN CALLED.

Begin training "recall" with your puppy on the leash—it will be simpler to introduce the new command this way. Have a treat in your hand and bring it to his nose. Say the puppy's name and use a cue word, for example, "come." ("Recall" is one of the few commands that you can teach with a cue word immediately.) Back away a few steps; the puppy will be encouraged to go with you by the treat in your hand. As soon as he comes to you, slip your finger under his collar and click-and-treat. Practice this regularly until the puppy seems to know what is required, and then you can try "recall" off the leash. This time, ask someone else to hold your puppy while you

PUPPY TIP: DISTANCE

When you start practicing "recall," keep fairly close to your puppy so he doesn't have far to go to get to you, and then steadily increase the distance over time as he improves. If your puppy seems to forget what to do or is distracted and doesn't come to you, try it again from a much closer distance, and then steadily increase the distance again, as before.

move a few paces away. Call him as before, and when he comes to you, always slip your finger in his collar at once, so you have a firm grasp, even if you plan to release him again, otherwise the puppy will bound away (*see* the step-by-step demonstrations, page 90).

Make sure that the puppy always sees "recall" as a good thing, earning treats and lots of praise when he gets it right. Remember that you are always pleased to see your puppy, however long it has taken him to come. If he has taken his time, do not be angry, but just be less effusive with your praise and withhold the treat. When he comes quickly, reward him with a jackpot of treats.

Practice this frequently. Call your puppy to you often and in as many different situations as possible; for example, around the house, from the yard, or while on walks. Unless you vary the situation, the puppy will associate recall only when he is, for example, playing in the yard but not when he is running around with other puppies in the park.

Above Practice "recall" often and in a variety of places, so that your puppy learns to associate it with a wide variety of different situations.

Get others involved

Make sure all your family members can successfully call the puppy. You can even encourage neighbors to help you. This is a form of training that children can help out with and one that they will enjoy. It also ensures that they maintain control over the pup.

Involve a friend or family member (adult or child) playing the "go to" game—taking turns to call and treat your puppy so that he runs back and forth between you, responding to his name. This reinforces the response and also makes it into a game for the puppy. You can now extend this by playing the "go to" game between several members of the family. Dad calls, Mom calls, Susie calls, Billy calls, and so on, so that the puppy runs between all of you. Bear in mind that coming back to you must always be a pleasant experience, so use click-and-treat and praise every time.

Over the weeks, as your puppy becomes more advanced, try the recall during play sessions when other puppy owners are around, for example, at puppy school or when playing in the park. Call your puppy to you and put your finger in his collar, use click-and-treat, and then release him to play again. If your puppy does not come, all owners should return to their puppy and stop play until the recall is successful.

Don't just call your puppy to put his leash back on. Think puppy psychology—what does the puppy perceive as being rewarding, and what

Give lots of treats, praise, and affection to help your puppy form positive associations with "recall." It will make him more responsive to learning this command.

does he perceive as being unpleasant? If the puppy is playing freely, the reward is the freedom. If you call and put his leash on to go home, the freedom's gone. Your puppy doesn't want that, so he will become increasingly reluctant to come to you when you call.

To avoid this problem, call the puppy to you regularly when he is playing freely. Treat him, praise him, stroke him, and then let him go and play again. The puppy will enjoy being recalled because he will associate it with rewarding things—treats and praise, followed by more freedom to play. This way, when you finally call the puppy and put the leash on him, it won't seem so bad. Later on, even though your puppy has been coming back to you regularly, you may find he suddenly stops responding every time. This problem is dealt with later in this chapter (*see* Flight instinct, page 92.)

"COME TO ME"

You can play an extended version of the "go to" game at puppy school. Give your puppy to someone else to hold. Show your puppy your treat, then turn around and run a short distance away, turn and call "[puppy's name] come." When your puppy comes, put your finger in his collar, click-and-treat, and give lots of praise.

Recall: On the leash

INITIALLY, IT WILL BE FAR EASIER TO TEACH "RECALL" TO YOUR PUPPY WHILE HE IS ON THE LEASH. THIS HELPS YOUR DOG TO LEARN WHAT THE "RECALL" CUE WORD MEANS AND ALSO ENABLES YOU TO CREATE AN ATMOSPHERE IN WHICH YOUR PUP WILL LEARN TO ASSOCIATE "RECALL" WITH BEING CLOSE TO YOU, SO THAT HE COMES TO YOU WHEN YOU CALL.

Start with your puppy on a loose leash in a standing position. Use a food treat to lure him into going with you. Call the puppy's name and say the cue word ("come") so that he will learn the association between the word and the action.

It is not a good idea to let your puppy walk around with the leash dragging along—he could trip over it and injure himself, which will create a negative association with "recall," thereby stunting his learning process.

▼ Step 1

With your puppy on a loose leash and facing you, show him a food treat in your hand.

▼ Step 2

Back away, still showing your puppy the treat, saying your puppy's name and the "recall" cue word.

RECALL: ON THE LEASH

When teaching "recall" to your pup, ensure that you use both the cue word (for example, "come" or "here") and your puppy's name. Avoid using only his name because he hears it hundreds of times a day and won't know how you want him to respond. By teaching your puppy a "recall" word while he is on the leash, he will learn that when he hears it, he should be close to you. So, when you let him off the leash and he is away from you, he hears the "recall" word and knows to return to you. Many people mistakenly think that if they let their pup go, he will automatically know what to do when they call him back. But if a pup hasn't been taught a "recall" word and command he will never know what his owner requires of him. "Recall" is taught to create a closeness with your puppy within which he associates the "recall" word with the action.

▼ Step 3

The puppy will go with you, following the treat in your hand.

▼ Step 4

After you have backed away for two to three steps, click, and reward your puppy with the treat and lots of praise, so that he knows he has performed the command correctly.

Recall: Off the leash

GETTING YOUR PUPPY TO COME TO YOU WHEN HE IS OFF THE LEASH IS ONE OF THE MOST VALUABLE RESPONSES YOU CAN TEACH, AND SO IT IS WELL WORTH PRACTICING THIS AS OFTEN AS POSSIBLE. CALL YOUR PUPPY REGULARLY WHEN HE IS PLAYING AROUND THE HOUSE OR IN THE YARD, AND IT WILL SOON BECOME SECOND NATURE.

As with all other training, the "recall" cue word needs to stimulate a conditioned response in your puppy. Until this response is firmly conditioned, it would be better not to use the cue word if the pup is still unlikely to come back to you when called, for example, when he is playing a boisterous game with other dogs.

▼ Step 1

With your puppy off the leash and being held by someone else, show the pup a food treat.

▼ Step 2

Move a small distance away from your puppy, and then call "[puppy's name], come." (You can increase the distance steadily as your puppy's recall improves.)

RECALL: OFF THE LEASH

As your puppy becomes more advanced in learning "recall," you will try the command during play sessions when other puppy owners are around, for example, at puppy school or in the park. Call your puppy and put your finger in his collar, use click-and-treat, and then release him to continue playing. If he does not come, ask all the owners to return to their puppies and stop play until the recall is successful. You can easily play another version of this. Ask someone else to hold your dog, and then show the pup a food treat in your hand. Turn around and run a short distance away, turn and call, "[puppy's name] come!" When your puppy comes, put your finger in his collar, use click-and-treat, and give lots of warm praise.

▼ Step 3

Crouch down, smile warmly, and use the food lure to draw your puppy in close.

▼ Step 4

When he comes to you, put your finger in his collar, and click and treat. Call him regularly from the yard or on walks. Don't always wait until you want to put his leash on! Coming to you should always be a pleasant experience, so use click-and-treat and praise him every time.

Flight instinct

FROM THE AGE OF FIVE MONTHS ONWARD, PUPPIES GROW MORE
CONFIDENT AND INDEPENDENT. COUPLED WITH THEIR INSTINCTIVE
CURIOSITY AND NATURAL HORMONAL ACTIVITY, THIS MAY RESULT IN
BEHAVIOR THAT RESEMBLES DISOBEDIENCE.

There is another stage in a young puppy's life that owners should be aware of if he starts to show signs of disobedient behavior. A very young puppy is usually eager to stay around his owner. Your presence gives him confidence and security, so "recall" is not normally a problem at this time. But from the age of about five months onward, puppies start showing the physical and mental signs that they are maturing and growing into adolescence. They suddenly become more independent, and you may find that a previously fairly obedient puppy does not come when called. This stage in the puppy's development is called the "flight instinct period." Some animal experts link this period to that of young wolves who are old enough to start learning about hunting and want to begin fending for themselves. With domestic dogs, this period usually lasts from two to four weeks.

It is important to recognize the signs when they occur and to act appropriately. If the owner does not deal with this situation promptly, the puppy may come to think that coming when called is optional. If a puppy who has previously responded to recall is playing in the yard (for example) and fails to come when called, that is the time to act.

Take the puppy for walks regularly, as before, but the next time you let him play, keep the puppy on a very long leash. There are long leashes designed especially for this purpose, or you could simply use a clothes line. Call your puppy to you regularly. If he comes, feed him, praise him, and then let him go and play again. If he doesn't come when called, encourage him using a friendly voice, hand gestures, squeaky toys, and, if necessary, use a gentle hand-over-hand pull to take up the slack on the leash and restrict his movements. Don't jerk the leash or drag the puppy to you.

The very fact that his freedom is being restricted to some extent is sufficient to give the puppy the message. For the next two weeks, use the long leash every time the puppy is playing outside, and continue to call him regularly. He is most likely to ignore your call when he is distracted by more interesting sights, sounds,

REASONS FOR RECALL PROBLEMS

■ In addition to the "flight instinct period," there are other reasons why your puppy may not want to come when called. You will find your puppy's recall skills are much better if you can try to avoid these situations and continue to call your puppy for "nice" reasons, such as a treat, to be fussed over, and for games. Sometimes a puppy won't return if he was:

■ Previously scolded or punished for returning too slowly.
■ Recalled for something he perceived to be unpleasant, such as having his nails clipped.
■ Always recalled to have his leash put on.
■ Distracted by a new and interesting sight or smell.
■ Doing something more enjoyable, such as playing with other puppies.
■ In a new and disturbing situation, such as first day at puppy school.

If your puppy is at the flight instinct stage, keep taking him for regular walks, but keep him on an extended leash and practice calling him.

and smells. Make yourself more interesting to your puppy than all other distractions. Try taking a favorite toy and play with him, changing direction and/or hiding behind a tree. He should realize that he should watch you or you'll get lost. When hiding, ensure that you can always see your puppy, even though he can't see you, otherwise he may go off in the wrong direction. If you are out in a group, ask different members to hide and teach the puppy to find them. Keep it simple initially, increasing difficulty as his skill improves.

During this period, take your puppy to as many places as possible, eventually building up the level of distraction, until you are satisfied that he will come when called, regardless of what is going on around him. If he comes to you reluctantly or after a delay, offer moderate praise but don't give him a treat. Rapturous praise and treats should be reserved for those times your puppy comes to you promptly when you call.

When you feel that sufficient progress has been made, usually after about two weeks, go to a safe place, let the puppy off the leash, and tell him to go and "play." Give him time to play and run around, then call the puppy. If he comes quickly, he should be rewarded with a jackpot of treats and lots of warm praise and petting. If he comes more slowly, he should be praised quietly just for coming eventually, but without the treats and effusive words. If the puppy still doesn't come, use the long leash again for the next couple of days and repeat the exercise. Most puppies get over this phase after two weeks—but in some cases it can take as long as a month. Some puppies don't go through this phase at all. If you put in the time and commitment now, the recall will remain extremely good—even if not entirely perfect. But if you don't train the puppy now, you will find that in the future, he will think that "come" is optional and you'll have a major task ahead of you in retraining him to obey you.

Improving and troubleshooting

ONCE YOU GET INTO THE ROUTINE OF REGULAR TRAINING SESSIONS, YOU SHOULD SEE A STEADY IMPROVEMENT IN YOUR PUPPY'S RESPONSE. KEEP AT IT, BUT WATCH OUT FOR EARLY SIGNS OF PROBLEM BEHAVIOR PATTERNS AND TACKLE THEM NOW, BEFORE THEY BECOME TOO FIRMLY ENTRENCHED.

Make sure that you practice all the training instructions on a regular basis. Don't be tempted to think that because your puppy has "mastered" one form of activity, you only need to use it when necessary. Regular reinforcement of all the instructions you are teaching is the only way to ensure progress. Avoid making specific times of the day "training times" or always training him in the same place, or your puppy may think that your instructions only apply at those times and at that location.

Now that the initial novelty of owning a puppy may be wearing off, you may be finding that other members of the household, especially children, may be showing less inclination to help with puppy training. Nonetheless, you should continue to encourage all members of the family to spend time teaching the pup, both to enhance his understanding and to maintain control.

The "yo-yo" principle

As your puppy gets better at following your instructions, aim to vary the reinforcement by getting two, three, or even four responses for one reward, using the "yo-yo" principle. For example, first click-and-treat several "sits," but then only reward the second or third "sit." Then click-and-treat several more responses, and so on, so that gradually you are getting more and more "sits" without having to reward each one. When you want to increase the time the puppy remains in

the "sit" position, do several that you click-and-treat straight away, and then withhold the click for a few seconds. Then click-and-treat a few straightaway again and so on, gradually building up the time in seconds. This helps to reinforce the puppy's training. However, do not reward him if he moves before you have clicked. Gradually, you can raise your standards by rewarding only the best responses (for example, the fastest "sit," the best "watch me," the longest "stay"), but remember to praise them all!

When you integrate a new behavior into your puppy's repertoire, make sure that you continue to repeat the commands he's already learned. Puppies are usually eager to respond to the most recent lessons, so it is important to get the puppy to repeat what he has previously learned. Clicker training encourages your puppy to think for himself, so, while he is learning, he is likely to experiment by offering you previous responses that have been rewarded. This is one of the things that makes clicker training so fascinating. Don't worry about this experimenting. Relax and enjoy it! Just don't reward what you haven't asked for.

You may find that your puppy seems more responsive on some days than on others and may even seem to have forgotten an instruction that he had previously been following perfectly. This can be extremely frustrating, but it is vitally important that you do not lose your temper.

Your puppy won't understand why you are angry and may appear even more uncooperative. Patience with your puppy is as important now as when you first started training him. Just like humans, puppies can have their "off days," and their lack of response should not be interpreted as stubbornness or disobedience. It may be that your puppy is tired or slightly unwell, for example, he could be struggling with a teething discomfort. In this type of situation, rather reduce your standards or give him a "day off" and just play with him. Perhaps he could be bored, in which case you could try introducing more movement-based activities into your training sessions—for example, sometimes throw the treat for him to go after, instead of giving it to him, or reward him with a game or favorite toy. Be very careful in dealing with your puppy at times like these because showing disapproval when he could be off-color, or simply tired and bored, could send a very confusing message to your pup, when all he wants is your approval.

Regular practice with your puppy in different places and at different times during the day is the best way to reinforce training instructions.

Following: On the leash

GETTING YOUR PUPPY TO FOLLOW YOU, ON AND OFF THE LEASH, REQUIRES A LOT OF TIME AND PATIENCE. BUT THE DEGREE OF CONTROL YOU WILL ACHIEVE OVER YOUR PUPPY, ESPECIALLY WHEN YOU ARE OUTDOORS WALKING AMONG STRANGERS, WILL AMPLY REWARD ALL THE EFFORT AND PERSEVERANCE YOU PUT IN NOW.

Your puppy must learn that if he pulls, you will always stand still and no forward progress will be made, but that if the leash is loose he will continue on his walk, which is what he wants. If you haven't got time to leash train properly because you are in a hurry to get somewhere, try using a harness instead of a collar. This will help your puppy to learn that pulling on a harness is fine, but pulling on a collar doesn't work because it makes you stop and stand still.

Step 1

With your puppy on a loose leash, show him that you have a treat in your hand, while keeping the clicker handy, too. Call his name and take two, three, or four steps at a time, and click-and-treat whenever the puppy is walking near you. Keep your hand close to your body; avoid swinging it or holding it too high, which will only encourage the puppy to jump up.

Step 2

Your puppy should be following you. When necessary, encourage him to walk in the right direction by talking to him and tapping your leg. If he pulls ahead, stand still, regain his attention, and change direction.

FOLLOWING: ON THE LEASH

Even though your puppy will follow on the leash more easily if he is first taught off the leash, leash training still requires consistency, time, and patience. Pressure invites counter-pressure, so if you keep pulling in one direction, your puppy will simply pull in the opposite direction, and before too long you'll both be in a gridlock. The obvious solution is always to make sure that the leash is loose. To do this, speak in a "happy" voice to encourage your pup to follow you, and initially use the clicker, treats, and praise when the leash is loose. If he pulls, stand still, get his attention, and then set off again with the leash loose. Your puppy should learn that when he pulls and the leash is tight, he will not get anywhere at all, but if the leash stays loose, he'll keep walking. As he gets the idea, you can phase out the rewards, and use only praise.

▼ Step 3

Once he is following close to you again, click and treat. You could also click while you are still moving and the pup is close to you, and then stop before you treat, if this is easier for you.

▼ Step 4

With time and patience, rewards, and praise, your pup will soon be walking comfortably on the leash.

Following: Off the leash

TEACH YOUR PUPPY TO WALK WITH YOU—BOTH OFF THE LEASH AND ON A LOOSE LEASH—INSTEAD OF PULLING YOU ALONG. IT CAN MAKE ALL THE DIFFERENCE BETWEEN A WALK THAT IS ENJOYABLE AND ONE THAT FEELS LIKE AN UNPLEASANT CHORE.

Begin without a leash and get your puppy to follow you around the house and yard. His reward for staying close to you and keeping at your pace is to get tidbits and praise. Use plenty of encouraging words and practice regularly. Once your pup is following you without a leash, try walking him around the house and yard, but this time on a leash. Don't get into the habit of pulling on his leash to get him to follow you. With time and patience, the puppy will learn to follow you, regardless of whether or not he is on the leash.

Time your clicks

When the puppy is walking beside you on a loose leash, reward him by clicking, treating, and praising. This way the puppy will come to understand that he is being rewarded for walking with you, with the leash loose. Practice this

The secret to mastering leash work is really to practice as much as you can, in as many different situations as possible.

Be careful to have only your puppy off the leash in safe areas—it can be very easy for a curious puppy to get into a sticky situation.

frequently—around four or five times a day, if you have time—first around the house and yard, and then up and down the sidewalk outside.

Always bear in mind that the main purpose of the leash is to act as an additional security measure when you are walking your puppy in public, especially near traffic or when there are other dogs around. Its purpose is not to slow the puppy down if he is walking too fast, nor to pull the puppy along if he is trailing behind. In fact, that would be counterproductive. Puppies (and older dogs) automatically lean forward whenever they feel pressure against their neck or chest. Owners inadvertently reinforce this reflex response if they continue to move forward while pulling back on the leash, or if they jerk the leash to get the puppy to follow when he has stopped.

PUPPY TIP: DRIVE, DON'T WALK

If you are going to a place, such as the park, where your puppy is going to be let off the leash, try to go there in the your car rather than on foot, at least until he has mastered following on the leash. This way the puppy won't associate walking on the leash with being released and allowed to play. Otherwise, he may get into the habit of pulling on the leash in his excitement to get there quickly.

WHY DO DOGS PULL?

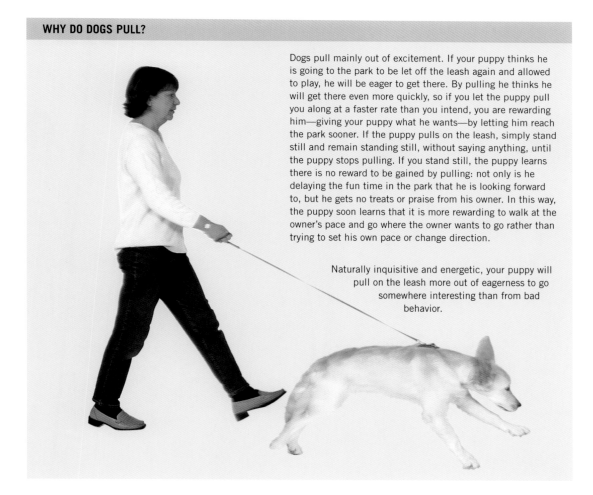

Dogs pull mainly out of excitement. If your puppy thinks he is going to the park to be let off the leash again and allowed to play, he will be eager to get there. By pulling he thinks he will get there even more quickly, so if you let the puppy pull you along at a faster rate than you intend, you are rewarding him—giving your puppy what he wants—by letting him reach the park sooner. If the puppy pulls on the leash, simply stand still and remain standing still, without saying anything, until the puppy stops pulling. If you stand still, the puppy learns there is no reward to be gained by pulling: not only is he delaying the fun time in the park that he is looking forward to, but he gets no treats or praise from his owner. In this way, the puppy soon learns that it is more rewarding to walk at the owner's pace and go where the owner wants to go rather than trying to set his own pace or change direction.

Naturally inquisitive and energetic, your puppy will pull on the leash more out of eagerness to go somewhere interesting than from bad behavior.

Following: Figure eight

THIS IS A GREAT EXERCISE FOR HELPING YOUR PUPPY TO IMPROVE HIS
COORDINATION. IT ALSO TEACHES HIM TO FOCUS ON WHAT YOU ARE DOING.
YOU NEED TWO OBJECTS OR CHAIRS FOR BEACONS WHEN YOU CREATE THE
COURSE FOR DOING FIGURE EIGHT.

This exercise teaches your puppy to watch what
you are doing. You should walk at the same
speed at all points on the course and encourage
your puppy to keep up with you when he is on

the outer edge of the eight course. When he is on
the inside, you need to teach him to swivel his
hind legs slightly backward and to slow down, so
that he drops back to keep up with you.

▼ Step 1

Begin at the central point between
the two beacons, show your puppy a
treat in your hand, and keep the
clicker handy.

▼ Step 2

With the pup on your left side, set
off around the beacon on your right,
so that the puppy will be on the
outside of the figure eight. He will
need to move faster than you to
keep up, but encourage him to
stay with you.

▼ Step 3

Then return through the midpoint
between the beacons, and walk,
turning counterclockwise, around
the other beacon.

The mobility of the canine physique is orientated around the front legs. In this respect, dogs are "unaware" of their hind legs. Owners can use the left-hand circles in the figure eight exercise to help their dogs gain coordination in their hind legs. Dogs have a strong sense of visual orientation, and when walking beside you, they are highly aware of the direction your body is facing. If you have encouraged your pup to look at you, then when you turn the top half of your body toward him, it will teach him to move backward, thereby introducing his hind legs as the pivot of the movement. Through awareness of his physical orientation to you, your puppy's movement will become more aligned with yours, making leash work much easier.

▼ Step 4

Now teach your puppy to swivel his hind legs slightly backward by getting him to look at you, and turn the top half of your body toward him. At the same time, move your hand holding the treat slightly backward on your left, so that the pup drops back to keep up with you.

▼ Step 5

Practice this several times, giving clicks and rewards when necessary. Click when the leash is loose, and gradually phase out rewards and use only praise. Soon your pup will follow you on a complete circuit for only one click-and-treat.

▼ Step 6

Gradually, you can increase the number of times you complete the circuit, and then just click-and-treat at the end.

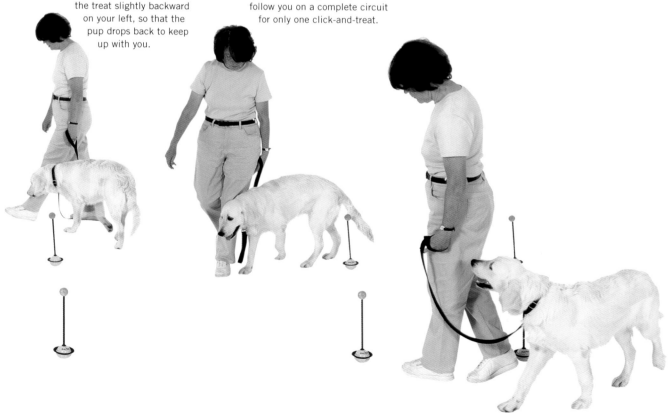

Meet and play with other dogs

IT IS IMPORTANT FOR YOUR PUPPY'S DEVELOPMENT THAT HE HAS THE OPPORTUNITY TO MEET AND PLAY WITH OTHER PUPPIES OF A SIMILAR AGE. THIS SHOULD START BEFORE THE AGE OF TWENTY WEEKS, SINCE AT THAT AGE DOGS ENTER A NEW STAGE OF MATURITY AND THERE IS A CHANGE IN THE WAY THEY INTERACT AND PLAY.

▶ Step 1

Ask your puppies for a "sit"; then reward them by removing their leashes and let them go off to play. When you are out with your puppy, make sure that he returns to you first before he starts play. Letting him go without "checking in" with you, leads to undisciplined behavior. Making your pup aware of you will also give him a greater sense of security.

▶ Step 2

Notice how the dogs curve their bodies when they approach each other. It is canine etiquette not to meet head-on. First acquaintances are made through light sniffing of each other.

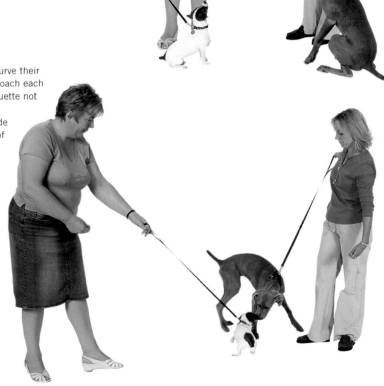

MEET AND PLAY WITH OTHER DOGS

Puppies need a variety of experience and stimulation, as well as the opportunity to discover their surroundings. Owners that are overly protective and reluctant to let their puppies run around and play risk ending up with an adult dog that is afraid and unable to cope—even with things like bumpy terrain—because he hasn't had enough exposure to the world. It can also be detrimental to a puppy's social development, leaving him unable to communicate with his own kind because he has been deprived of their company. So, the mature dog will be insecure about visiting strange places and meeting new dogs.

▶ *Step 3*

The dogs continue their mutual sniffing, moving around each other in circular movements, instead of making direct advances.

PUPPIES LEARN THROUGH PLAY!

Meeting and playing helps puppies to learn vital behavior lessons, such as bite inhibition, canine body language, and calming signals. They also learn about the pecking order in the pack and build the social and physical confidence they need to interact with other dogs.

▼ *Step 4*

Observe how the larger dog has lowered his head, so that both dogs are on a level footing with each other. This shows that neither feels threatened or hostile, and that play is about to begin.

▼ *Step 5*

Having made their introductions, the puppies get into the rough-and-tumble of play.

Meet and greet people

YOU AND YOUR PUPPY WILL MEET MANY PEOPLE, SOME OF WHOM HAVE
DOGS. WHEN YOU ARE OUT AND ABOUT, IT IS IMPORTANT THAT YOUR
PUPPY LEARNS TO TAKE THESE ENCOUNTERS IN HIS STRIDE, SO THAT HE
REMAINS UNDER CONTROL AND IS NEITHER FEARFUL NOR OVEREXCITED.

You can extend leash training and enhance your control over your puppy by practicing an exercise called "meet and greet." At puppy school, we start by meeting a "stranger" (that is, someone your puppy is unfamiliar with)—someone who doesn't have a dog with them. Instruct your puppy to "sit" while you greet the "new" acquaintance. Chat briefly, and then click-and-treat and praise the puppy before moving on. Aim to do this regularly when you see someone you know while you're out walking your dog.

We then move on to include other puppy owners in your "meet and greet," asking you to imagine that you had just met the other owner

▼ Step 1

When you draw near, keep the leash loose and allow the pups to "curve" as they approach each other.

▼ Step 2

As you meet, let the puppies make their acquaintances, through sniffing each other briefly, before asking for a "sit."

and his or her puppy while taking your own puppy for a walk. The two owners exchange greetings while the puppies sit quietly. Practice this with a puppy-owning neighbor or someone you met at puppy school. Make "meet and greet" a regular part of your training routine.

Take care when the two puppies walk toward each other that they do not approach head to head. It reduces the chances of the encounter leading to a playful rough and tumble, which may make gaining control difficult. In normal circumstances, it is basic canine etiquette for dogs to avoid meeting head on, as this is perceived as a threatening act. Instead, allow the puppies to approach slightly to one side, keeping the leashes loose. Stand still so that,

if they choose to, the puppies can turn and sniff each other.

At puppy school, we arrange it so that everyone meets at least four other owners and puppies and follows the same routine—get the puppy to sit, chat with the other owner, praise the puppy and click-and-treat—then move on. Over time, you should extend the period that your puppy sits while you talk to the other owner.

TIP: DISTRACTION

If your puppy starts to play too boisterously with another dog, the best way to separate the two animals is to use a food lure. Simply place a treat on your pup's nose and use it to draw him away.

Step 3

With the dogs under control, their owners can greet each other without worrying that their pets will start to misbehave. Seeing the extended hands, the puppy on the left here is looking for any hand signals.

Step 4

Rewarding the dogs when they behave well helps to reinforce the training process. It is equally important that the dogs do not start to become excitable at this stage, and they should only be encouraged to walk on again when a verbal command to do so is given.

5 Further training

As part of your puppy's early training and socialization, it is very important that he has the opportunity to learn how to get along with other people and other animals. This chapter explains how you can help your pup to socialize comfortably with other adults, children, and animals. There are also several new commands for further training that you can teach your dog over time, as he continues his education.

Down from stand

THIS IS A GOOD EXERCISE TO TEACH YOUR DOG FOR THE PURPOSE OF
TRAINING. HAVING LEARNED "SIT" BEFORE "DOWN," HE MAY THINK THAT
HE SHOULD ALWAYS SIT BEFORE LYING DOWN. THIS TECHNIQUE TEACHES
HIM HOW TO LIE DOWN DIRECTLY FROM A STANDING POSITION.

Initially, you taught your dog to lie down by
getting him to sit first, and then using a treat to
lure him into "down." Along with the cue word,
that particular movement of your hand will have
become the puppy's signal for "down." For this
exercise you will start by using the same cue
word and hand signal, but with your dog in a
"stand,"position so that he will learn how to
apply his association with the command to a
different situation.

▽ Step 1

Start with your dog in a standing
position, facing you. Show him that
you have a treat, and hold it slightly
below his nose.

▽ Step 2

Lower your hand straight down, and
then slowly sweep it forward along
the floor space in front of your dog,
and give the cue word for "down."

Ideally, you will want your puppy to learn to drop into "down" without having to sit first. Sometimes your dog may think that "sit" is actually part of the "down" behavior and when you show him the treat he could go into a "sit" immediately. This can be rectified if, when you begin the exercise with the dog standing, you make sure that you hold your hand slightly lower than his nose as you show him the treat. If you are not specific about this, he will be confused about what you want him to do. Remember, if you bring the treat up any higher than nose level, your dog will associate this with a "sit" command.

Step 3

Your dog will have recognized the signal because you taught him "down" from "sit," and will drop directly into a "down," following the lure of the treat.

Step 4

Once he is successfully in "down," click-and-treat and give your dog lots of warm praise and affection.

Stand from down

BEING ABLE TO PERFORM A VARIETY OF POSITION CHANGES WILL ENHANCE YOUR DOG'S TRAINING, ESPECIALLY IF YOU LATER PROGRESS TO COMPETITIVE OBEDIENCE, WHERE COMMANDS SUCH AS THIS ARE NECESSARY FOR GOOD DISTANCE CONTROL.

Having taught your dog "stand" from the "sit" position, he will know the cue word for this command. Now he can learn to stand from a "down." By broadening the range of exercises that you teach him, your dog will use more of his mental capacity. It will also help to strengthen his focus on you.

▶ Step 1

With your dog in the "down" position, show him a food treat in your hand, holding it slightly above and forward from nose level.

◀ Step 2

Slowly bring your hand up and forward, using your cue word for "stand." Lured by the treat, your dog should rise to follow it. Be careful to bring the treat forward (that is, toward you) and don't raise it up too high, or your dog could go straight into a "sit."

At first, your dog may appear confused and not understand that you are teaching him a different technique of getting into "stand." Since you have already taught him the cue word for "stand," allow your dog time to register that you are using the same cue word for this exercise. You will later teach him also to sit from a "down," and it is crucial that you use the correct hand signals for these different commands, so that he will be able to distinguish what you want from the direction and position of your hand movement.

Step 3

Once your dog has completed the movement into the standing position, click and give him the treat, so he knows he has given the correct response to your command.

Step 4

Regular practice will reinforce this new command as part of your dog's behavior. As with all training, gradually phase out clicks and treats. Always give warm praise when he does things right.

Sit from down

THIS EXERCISE WILL TEACH YOUR DOG AN ALTERNATIVE WAY OF GETTING INTO A SITTING POSITION—DIRECTLY FROM A "DOWN," WITHOUT FIRST GOING INTO "STAND." TEACHING HIM THESE DIFFERENT POSITION CHANGES WILL STIMULATE YOUR DOG'S MIND AND MAKE HIM THINK, SO THIS IS WORTH TEACHING.

Your dog will already know the cue word for "sit," although he has learned the behavior from a standing position. As with the previous exercise, the correct use of the appropriate hand signal is the key to teaching your dog this movement successfully. Do not bring your hand too far forward, and take it slowly, because he might be confused into standing or even jumping up.

▼ Step 1

Beginning with your dog in "down," bring your hand holding a food treat to just above his nose.

▼ Step 2

Slowly raise your hand up and backward over the dog's head, saying the cue word as you do this.

SIT FROM DOWN

Getting your dog to sit reliably, whether from a "stand" or a "down," requires that you are very clear and unambiguous about helping him to understand that you are using the same cue word, but in a different way. Remember: the essence of all good and successful puppy training is constant repetition. It is vital that you keep on repeating the behaviors until your pup has the correct associations firmly established in his mind. Since it is easy for him to become confused when you are teaching him a variation of something he already knows, try to work together in a peaceful and quiet place where you can avoid interruptions— you don't want your puppy to be distracted by a group of boisterous children, ringing telephones, or other dogs barking.

 Step 3

The dog rises onto his front legs as his head follows the food treat, bringing him into a "sit." Click-and-treat as soon as he has responded correctly.

 Step 4

With patience and consistent practice, your dog will soon understand how you are using the cue word and hand signal for achieving "sit" in this way. Be sure to reward him with treats and warm praise.

 # Stay

IN THIS EXERCISE YOU WILL TEACH YOUR DOG TO STAY IN THE POSITION
YOU HAVE ASKED FOR UNTIL YOU TELL HIM THAT HE CAN MOVE, BY
USING A RELEASE WORD, FOR EXAMPLE, "OKAY" OR "THAT WILL DO."

Ultimately, the goal of this exercise is to be able to leave your dog in a "sit," "stand," or "down" position, walk away, and return a few minutes later to find your dog still in the same position. He must remain in that pose until you give your release word. Start by teaching your dog to "stay" when you are standing beside him, and then teach him to stay when you move away from him. "Stay" can be taught from a "sit," "stand," or "down" position.

▼ Step 1

Begin with your dog in a "down," and stand by him. Using a gentle hand gesture as your signal for "stay," count to five, and say the release word, followed by calm, but warm praise. Too much fuss could overexcite him, so that he does not "stay" until you give the release.

▼ Step 2

With your dog in "down," take up your position next to him, give your hand signal, then swivel around to face him. Continue to give the hand signal, count to five, swivel back, and then click-and-treat and release. Keep increasing the time during which you ask him to "stay."

The main problem that owners may encounter in teaching "stay" is that the dog moves before hearing the click, receiving the treat, and being released. Sometimes this happens because your have tried to progress too quickly, either by expecting the dog to stay too long or because you have moved too far away, at a stage when your dog just isn't steady enough. If your dog makes a mistake and moves too soon, simply re-position him and start again—at a shorter distance, for a shorter time. Try to remain calm and don't get angry. As with any exercise—if you feel you are getting frustrated, it is better to stop the training session (and have a break to restore your composure!)

Step 3

Get your dog to lie down, and then take a half step away from him, give the hand signal as you do this, and then return, click-and-treat, and release. Steadily increase the distance that you move away from your dog as you practice this, but always return to him before you click, treat, praise, and release.

Step 4

With your dog in the "down" position, you should now gradually stretch the time that you remain at a distance from him before returning, and then click and reward with treats and praise, then release.

Step 5

Eventually your dog will learn to maintain his position until you return, even when you go out of sight. The secret to your dog's mastering this command is constant repetition and reward, as well as the gradual increase of time and distance that you are away from him.

Leave it

THERE ARE MANY THINGS IN AND AROUND THE HOME THAT DOGS FIND ATTRACTIVE, AND WHICH WE WOULD PREFER FOR THEM TO IGNORE, FOR EXAMPLE, THAT SIZZLING STEAK ON THE KITCHEN TABLE, OR THE CAT YOU MEET WHEN OUT WALKING. "LEAVE IT" ENABLES YOU TO GET YOUR DOG TO REFRAIN FROM TAKING OBJECTS OR EATING FOOD THAT IS OFF-LIMITS.

By teaching "leave it" according to the following instructions, you will help your dog to form a positive association with the cue word. He will perceive "leave it" as a rewarding thing to do. It is not vital what position your dog is in, although he will probably sit. Asking him for a "sit" or a "down" while teaching this new behavior is likely to confuse his understanding of what you want.

▶ Step 1

With a food treat hidden inside your fist, offer your hand to your dog. He will sniff, and probably try to get the treat out of your fist.

◀ Step 2

Wait for your dog to withdraw from your hand and click immediately. The idea is for your dog to realize that when he withdraws his mouth from your fist, he will receive a reward.

It is well worth spending time on every stage of this exercise. Make sure that you don't try to progress too fast. For example, if you place the treat on the floor before the dog reliably understands the meaning of "leave it," and he grabs the treat before you can prevent him, he will have taken a huge backward step in his perception of what is required. The same is true of putting your own food on a plate at his level. Make sure, if he tries to grab the food, that you can get there before he does, otherwise you will have very effectively taught him to steal! At each phase, when the dog "leaves it" correctly, be sure that you always give the treat to the dog—NEVER allow him to take it.

▶ *Step 3*

Give him the treat from your fingertips. Do not offer it to him from your open palm. Once he reliably withdraws his mouth, add your cue word ("leave it") as he withdraws, and then click-and-treat. Repeat this many times to enable your dog to get the association between the cue word and his withdrawal from your hand. Also extend the time that you ask him to "leave it," and then reward.

◀ *Step 4*

With a treat on your open palm held at his nose level, tell your dog to "leave it." If he tries to take it, close your hand to prevent him, and repeat the step. Once he gets the idea and withdraws from your open palm, click and give him the treat—again with your fingertips. Gradually increase the length of time that passes before you click-and-treat.

(Continues on page 118)

Leave it (continued)

When teaching your dog to "leave it," remember that the cue words you plan to use should be something you will say only when you want the dog to refrain from taking something. Moreover, it should always be said in a firm, but pleasant tone of voice. Do not shout or become aggressive, otherwise your dog will automatically interpret this as disapproval and form negative associations with the cue word. Also, make thorough use of the clicker to let your dog know exactly when he has done what you wanted, and you should also use lots of praising words, such as "yes," "good," or "that will do." This type of reinforcement will help your dog to learn the behavior effectively, and in a positive way.

▼ Step 5

Sit in a chair or on the floor, and place a treat on your knee, telling the dog to "leave it" as he starts to sniff at it.

▼ Step 6

If he tries to take it, cover it with your hand, and begin again. When he makes the connection and withdraws, click and give him the treat. Keep extending the time before you click-and-treat.

LEAVE IT

Once your dog responds reliably and correctly whenever you say "leave it," start applying it to situations in real life. Start with simple situations, so that he can succeed easily—if you make it too difficult, he may become confused and not be able to "remember" the correct behavior you have taught him. Make a big fuss and give your dog lots of treats whenever he does this successfully. As your dog improves, start to use "leave it" in more challenging situations, for example, in places where there are distractions and it may be difficult to gain his attention. He may not get it right first time, but persist until he does and keep using tasty treats, so you can continue to teach him that "leave it" means he will be rewarded for NOT trying to take it.

Step 7

Progress to putting the treat in various places, for example, on your foot, on your dog's paw (see below), or on the floor. Click-and-treat immediately for every different place where he withdraws, and then steadily increase the periods of time as you continue. Transfer this training to other things, such as "leaving" a toy, which you can also reward by giving a click and then letting him play with the toy. It is also very important for your dog to learn to "leave" other things such as animal droppings.

Step 8

Try setting up learning situations at home or with friends. For example, put a plate of food on a low table. When your dog starts nosing around, give the "leave it" cue words, and click-and-treat as soon as he responds correctly. Give him lots of warm praise and rewards, so that he can know when he has done what you wanted.

Retrieve

"RETRIEVE" IS AN EXERCISE USED IN VARIOUS SITUATIONS. COMPETITIVE OBEDIENCE AND TRIALS REQUIRE THAT THE EXERCISE BE PERFORMED TO A VERY HIGH LEVEL OF PRECISION. HOWEVER, MANY DOGS THOROUGHLY ENJOY GAMES THAT INVOLVE RETRIEVING A BALL OR A TOY.

There are two distinct ways of teaching your dog to retrieve. It depends what you want from this exercise. You could just teach a "play retrieve" where the dog chases after a toy and learns that if he brings it back, you'll throw it again, and the games continue for as long as you wish. However, make sure that the game stops when you want it to, not when your dog has had enough (you are the one in control). You can also teach a "formal" retrieve, as set out below.

▶ Step 1

Teach your dog to hold the article to be retrieved by initially clicking-and-treating any interest that he displays when you show him the object, which could be something like a toy, a dumbbell, or even a piece of rubber pipe.

◀ Step 2

Gradually progress to expecting him to nose it before you click, treat, and praise. By working on this in stages, stalling the click-and-treat as you expect more of a response, he will eventually pick up the article.

RETRIEVE

Some dogs, such as gun dogs, tend to be "natural" retrievers, and generally will be easier to teach how to retrieve things. This exercise makes the dog use his mind and can benefit his coordination. It also involves the use of previously learned behaviors like "sit" and "wait." Dogs that enjoy retrieving when out on walks will get lots of healthy exercise from running back and forth, collecting a toy and returning it to their owners. If your dog tends to be more interested in other things than in you when out walking, getting him interested in playing retrieval games with you will teach him that all-important exercise of focussing in on you. He will grow less likely to run off after other dogs or distractions.

▶ ### Step 3

Encourage him to take the article in his mouth, until eventually he picks it up and holds it. Some dogs learn this very quickly, but others may take much longer. Try to be patient and enjoy watching him discover what is required. Work on this for brief periods at a time, or he may get bored.

◀ ### Step 4

Put the article in different places on the floor around you. Click-and-treat every time the dog picks it up and gives it to you. When he is doing this reliably, introduce the cue word ("fetch") as he goes to fetch the article. Increasing the distance every time, progress to throwing the article away from you. When he goes off to fetch it and brings it back, click and reward him with a treat.

(Continues on page 122.)

Retrieve (continued)

RETRIEVE

Dogs that are not natural retrievers may require a great deal of time and patience in order to learn what "retrieve" is all about—a challenge, if you enjoy one. For the non-retrievers, steps 1, 2, and 3 are the biggest hurdle to overcome, so try these tips: Use very special treats and initially click-and-treat any interest in the article quite a few times, and then withhold the click and wait for your dog to do something else. Through previous training exercises, he has learned that the presence of the clicker means there is a reward for the right behavior.

◀ ***Step 5***

With the dog sitting by your side, ask for a "wait" and make sure he can see the article in your hand.

▼ ***Step 6***

Throw the article a short distance away and send him out to "fetch." When he returns with the article and gives it to you, click, and then give him a treat.

RETRIEVE

When teaching "retrieve," your dog will also realize that the click has something to do with the retrieve article, and he is likely to do something else, such as touch it with his nose or perhaps even pick it up in his mouth. Take whatever he offers you and click-and-treat several times before withholding the click again and waiting for him to try something else. It is a fascinating way of watching him learn. Eventually he really will pick up the article, willingly offer it to you, and even sit and wait. This may take some time to perfect—after all, your puppy is handing over his favorite toy—so don't give up!

▽ Step 7

As you progress, you will be able to teach your dog to sit and wait (without holding his collar) until you tell him to "fetch." You can also teach him to return by coming to sit in front of you and holding the article in his mouth until you take it from him. When you first try the latter part of the exercise, he may drop the article and then sit. If he does, as a separate exercise, teach your dog to sit while holding the article in his mouth (see Step 8.)

▽ Step 8

You will have taught him earlier to hold the article in his mouth, so ask your dog for a "sit," and then encourage him to take the article in his mouth, and hold it for increasing amounts of time (two seconds, five seconds, and so forth) by gradually holding back on the click-and-treat.

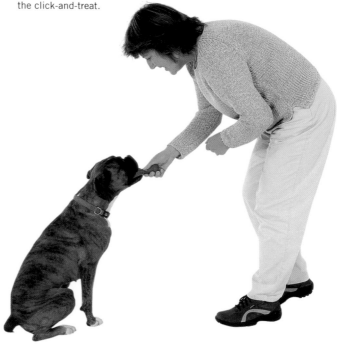

6 Out and about

As his world expands, your puppy's confidence will continue to grow. This chapter gives advice on where to take your puppy, and what experiences could prevent him from developing fears based on things, places, or persons that are unfamiliar or unpleasant to him. There are also tips on how to get your puppy used to car travel and how to manage any problems that may occur on the road. For those with active and intelligent breeds, there is a section on sporting and competitive activities that could be fun for both you and your pooch.

Puppies and people

NOW THAT YOUR PUPPY HAS SETTLED INTO HIS NEW HOME AND FAMILY, HE NEEDS TO BE INTRODUCED TO AS MANY DIFFERENT TYPES OF PEOPLE AS POSSIBLE. BEING UNFAMILIAR WITH SOMEONE'S APPEARANCE OR A NEW PLACE CAN BE INTIMIDATING FOR YOUR PUPPY, SO HELP HIM BUILD THE CONFIDENCE HE NEEDS TO COPE WITH OUR WORLD.

Socializing your puppy

In addition to integrating your puppy into your home life, it is vitally important that your puppy learns how to be friendly and sociable with other people and animals he may meet, and not just other dogs. Socialization is an ongoing process that is not just confined to puppy classes, but starts as soon as you bring your puppy home and introduce him to your family and any pets you may already have. Puppies have to make a sudden transition from the familiar comfort and security of their first home with their mothers and littermates and face the unfamiliar sights and sounds of their new environment. Some puppies may be confident and others may be shy, but, whatever their nature, they are all highly inquisitive. By exposing your pup to lots of new situations and unfamiliar people of all ages, and to other animals, you can make sure he develops the confidence he will need to live in our human environment.

Help your puppy's adjustment to his new environment by frequently exposing him to people of all shapes and sizes.

While the puppy is still very young is the time to take steps to prevent any socialization problems from occurring. You should take every opportunity to introduce your puppy to as many different people (and places—*see* page 132) as possible. Let your puppy meet people of all ages, occupations, and racial groups, so that he doesn't become intimidated by, or aggressive toward, anyone with whose appearance he is unfamiliar.

Getting comfortable with people

You should include older people using walking sticks and walkers, people in wheelchairs, people wearing glasses, and people in uniform, such as police officers, fire fighters, and soldiers. Introduce your puppy to the mailman and ask him to give your puppy a treat. Then, instead of barking and growling when your puppy sees him, your dog will think he is good news and greet him like an old friend.

Motorcycle riders and other people who wear helmets can seem particularly disturbing to older dogs that haven't been exposed to them when they were puppies. A dog could find it rather unsettling when the person suddenly removes the helmet—the animal thinks they've taken their

If you allow many different people to handle your puppy in gentle and calm ways, he will be relaxed and comfortable and will think of them as friends.

head off! A baby in a backpack can also seem strange to a puppy. They do not always see this as two separate individuals—an adult and an infant—but as a strange alien being with two heads! So make sure your pup sees both as often as you can.

Encourage different children to make a fuss of your puppy. Tell them to stroke the his chest or the side nearest to them, rather than starting with the head and back, which the puppy could find threatening.

Meeting children

It is especially important that your puppy has plenty of contact with children. Many puppy classes encourage dog owners to bring along their own children, or relatives' children, to class to meet the other young dogs. But it is also important that your puppy gets used to seeing children in his own home. If there are no children in your family, encourage relatives, neighbors, and friends to bring their children for a visit. Encourage the children to stroke the puppy gently and give him treats. This ensures that the puppy doesn't develop a fear of children, which, in turn, reduces the risk that the puppy will bite, even in play (a process known as "bite inhibition"—*see* page 73). There will then be far less chance that the dog, when older, becomes frightened in the presence of a child. If the

PUPPY TIP: TREATS

Keep a jar of your puppy's favorite treats by the front door for times when children come to call. Encourage the children to give your puppy a treat and stroke him. Your puppy will soon learn that children are good news and will look forward to meeting them, rather than shying away.

children are old enough, encourage them to tell the puppy to "sit" before playing (*see* page 80). This helps keep the child in control and also reinforces the puppy's training.

If your puppy doesn't meet children on a regular basis, you could put him on a leash and take him to your neighborhood park or school at play time (you may have to ask the school authorities for permission) and stay in the background with your puppy, letting him watch the children coming and going. The children don't need to stroke the puppy, although as long as you approve and supervise, they can if they wish. If necessary, he can just watch them from a short distance. The important thing is just to let the puppy see the children and get used to the way they look and sound so that your pet does not get frightened or overexcited when seeing a child.

Play sessions

Dogs are naturally social—and sociable— animals, so it is important that they have the opportunity to interact with one another on a regular basis. Most puppy classes include play sessions when the puppies can run around freely to meet the other pups and join in a little "rough and tumble." To avoid problems, it is important that the play sessions are kept tightly controlled—remember, even puppies can cause injury to themselves and other pups if things get out of hand. If there are a large number of puppies in the class, it is a good idea if only a

Teach your children to handle the puppy correctly, so that he feels secure and at ease whenever he is around them.

few puppies are let off the leash, at least in the initial stages. If the small and/or nervous puppies are released first, it will allow them the time and freedom to explore the room at their own pace and help them to lose some of their anxiety and shyness, and not get bowled over by the larger and more exuberant puppies!

If any of the puppies become too boisterous, the owners should go to their pups and spend a few moments calming them down, if necessary putting them on the leash for a short "time out." Once you have taught your puppy behaviors such as "sit" (*see* page 80), "watch me" (*see* page 78), and "recall" (*see* page 86), you will be able to incorporate them into your puppy's play sessions, not only at puppy classes but also when he is playing with other pups in the park.

For example, ask your puppy to "sit" or "watch me" before letting him off the leash to play. Periodically, go to your puppy, touch his collar, and ask for a "sit," give him a treat and make a fuss over him, and then say "go play." If you do this several times during a play session, it will help reinforce control over your puppy.

WARNING! STRANGE DOGS

Children must never approach a strange dog without the owner's permission. Having a puppy in the family may lull your child into a false sense of security regarding other people's dogs. So make sure your child always checks with the owner that a dog is safe to stroke. If there's any doubt, the child must keep away.

Children should only approach and play with dogs if they have the owner's permission and supervision.

Involving the children

CHILDREN AND PUPPIES USUALLY HAVE A GREAT TIME TOGETHER BECAUSE THEY ARE EQUALLY ENERGETIC, PLAYFUL, AND INQUISITIVE. HOWEVER, JUST AS YOUR PUPPY REQUIRES TRAINING, YOUR CHILDREN NEED TO BE TAUGHT HOW TO BEHAVE CORRECTLY AROUND PUPPIES AND OLDER DOGS.

Always be present to supervise when a child is interacting with a puppy. Never leave them alone together, because children sometimes become very excitable, which will only incite the puppy. These situations can often get out of hand, and a child may make the puppy feel threatened or accidentally injure him, which will leave him feeling anxious and insecure about being in the company of children.

Step 1

Stand directly behind the child so that he or she feels comfortable in the situation, and then give him or her a treat with which to get the puppy's attention.

Step 2

Show the child how to raise the treat to just above the puppy's eye level, so that the puppy will be lured into a "sit" position.

INVOLVING THE CHILDREN

Children and puppies generally have loads of fun together, but they can often get each other into trouble, especially when there are so many things around them that pose a potential danger—for example, electric cable, medication, machinery, appliances, and even toys. Try to ensure that their environment is as safe as possible. Never encourage children to play rough-and-tumble games with puppies and older dogs. Rather, get them to play games that stimulate brain activity, such as hide-and-seek or teaching tricks. Both kids and puppies should learn to play using brain instead of brawn.

Step 3

If the child struggles at first to get the puppy to sit by using the treat as a lure, you can step in and assist by using your cue word and hand signal.

Step 4

Once the exercise is completed, sit down with the child in your lap, and together give the puppy lots of warm praise, treats, and affection. This way, both puppy and child are forming positive associations about being in each other's company.

Exploring the big wide world

THE WORLD IS A BIG AND POTENTIALLY FRIGHTENING PLACE FOR A PUPPY. BUT IF YOU TAKE HIM OUT AND ABOUT NOW AND INTRODUCE HIM TO A VARIETY OF PLACES, PEOPLE, AND EXPERIENCES, AS HE GROWS OLDER HE WILL NOT DEVELOP THE FEARS—AND AGGRESSIVE TENDENCIES—THAT CAN OCCUR WHEN A DOG IS SUDDENLY CONFRONTED WITH THE UNKNOWN.

While your dog is still a puppy, it is essential that you take him to as many different places as he is allowed to go. At this stage in his life, he is highly receptive to new experiences and will enjoy the varied sights, sounds, and smells of everything the world has to offer. More importantly, if your puppy is introduced to a variety of new situations now, he is not so likely to be terrified of them later on. This is the approach that seeing-eye dog trainers use with their puppies, since it's essential that these dogs remain calm under any circumstance.

You could start by going out to explore your neighborhood. It may appear all too familiar to you, but to your puppy, it will be a fascinating place. Perhaps you could take him into your local stores (if they will allow it) or encourage some of the storeowners to come outside and say hello to him. Before you take him for long journeys in your car you will need to acclimate him to riding in it (see opposite).

Take your puppy to both urbanized areas and to rural settings. It is important for him to meet different animals and different sorts of people (see page 126) and that he gets used to having his paws on different surfaces, such as rough stones, grass, sand, and asphalt. Let him travel in trucks and vans and on boats, take him to the train station to watch the trains roar by. Some owners spend long periods standing with their puppy by the side of the road just watching the different vehicles go by.

You could walk him through revolving doors and let him ride in elevators. It's a good idea to take him to watch a sporting event, such as a tennis match—to see the players waving rackets around, or to a football game or youth-association soccer game, where there will be lots of children shouting at the top of their lungs. Dogs have sensitive hearing, so your pup needs to hear and get used to lots of different sounds while he is still receptive to new experiences, before he starts to develop a fear of them. Even the sound of people clapping in a large stadium or playing

Introducing your puppy to new sights and sounds will help build his confidence, so that he will be calm and confident in any situation with which he is familiar.

field, which we humans are used to, can come as a shock to a dog that has never heard it before.

All puppy owners need to be aware of the experiences that the puppies are having and to realize that everything that is done with them is a teaching situation. It is part of their education. When you are travelling with your dog, bear in mind the fear imprint period (see page 18.) If your puppy has a frightening experience during this period, the fear may stay with him and he will react badly every time he, for example, hears a particular sound or sees that sight, so it is really important that you handle it in the right way. Simply tell your dog in a calm voice that there is nothing to be afraid of, and then just walk away. Don't make a big fuss over your puppy—a mistake that many people tend to make—because this actually reinforces the fear.

On the road

Puppies are quite sensitive, and the unusual movement of the car can cause an upset tummy. To avoid these problems, try to introduce your pup to the vehicle slowly, in a way that makes it a fun experience.

Start off by sitting with your puppy in the car while it is parked in your driveway with the motor switched off. Have a toy with you and play with him. You could give him treats, or even feed him in the car, so that he associates your vehicle only with having a nice time. Now do the same thing with the car still stationary, but this time with the engine running.

Do this for only a few minutes to start off with, and then gradually build up the time. Now you could try driving your puppy to the end of your driveway, if the drive is long enough, or to the end of the road. Then take him around the block and on very short trips. When you are ready to take your puppy on a long trip in your car, don't feed him too soon before you go. If possible, feed

Placing a car crate in the rear of the vehicle not only keeps the puppy safe but also gives him a sense of security when he's in unfamiliar locations.

the puppy after but not before the journey. If you are unable to do this, try feeding your puppy at least two hours before your journey commences, but make sure that you stop regularly to give him enough opportunities to relieve himself comfortably. Always try to use some form of restraint to keep your puppy safe in the car. You could try a special harness, which fits into the seat belt, or you could use a dog guard or a crate to confine the puppy to the rear of the vehicle. Dogs should never sit on the front seat, since they cannot be easily restrained there. If the dog is likely to be a nuisance in the car, don't take him with you unless there is another adult sitting along with you. You can't drive your vehicle and control your puppy at the same time!

If barking is a problem, stop the car, if it is safe to do so, or pull over onto the curb and try to calm him down. But don't let the puppy out of the car for a run when he is barking. Otherwise, he will learn that when he barks and makes a noise he will be let out. You have to be aware of what the reward is for everything that your dog is doing. Alternatively, you could keep his crate in the vehicle and cover it with a blanket, since this can help comfort a puppy.

Future activities

ONCE YOUR PUPPY HAS MASTERED THE BASICS OF HIS TRAINING, YOU MAY WANT TO THINK ABOUT OTHER ACTIVITIES THAT YOU CAN TAKE PART IN ONCE YOUR DOG IS FULLY PHYSICALLY DEVELOPED, BOTH TO CONTINUE HIS EDUCATION AND TO MAINTAIN HIS INTEREST AND MOTIVATION.

Dog-training schools usually offer a range of classes for older dogs. These classes will often include activities with a competitive element, such as negotiating an obstacle course against the clock or being the first to fetch an object and return it to its owner. You can also practice these activities at home. You may find that your dog demonstrates a particular aptitude, skill, or enjoyment for certain activities that you wish to capitalize on. Collies are extremely agile and eager to learn activities such as negotiating an obstacle course and following instructions. Terriers enjoy activities involving running and chasing, especially with a ball.

Above Fetch is a fun game that your dog will enjoy and the whole family can take part in. But remember, a dog won't automatically bring back an item you've thrown. He is just as likely to run off with it! You will need to build up to this stage slowly by placing the ball or toy near you and then teaching your dog to pick it up and hand it to you. The techniques described in Chapter 5 can help with this. Then steadily increase the distance that you place the object until he knows to bring it back no matter how far away you throw it.

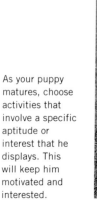

As your puppy matures, choose activities that involve a specific aptitude or interest that he displays. This will keep him motivated and interested.

WARNING! OVEREXERTION

Puppies have soft, fragile bones that are not yet fully formed, so they are easily damaged. Take care not to exercise them too fast or too far. The training activities shown in the step-by-step pages of this book are perfectly safe. However, agility exercises, especially those involving jumping and balance, should never be attempted before a dog is fully developed, at around eighteen months.

Sports and competition events

The following activities are for older dogs. If you want to make use of your dog's natural skills and would like to try out more advanced activities with him, there are numerous sports and pastimes for dogs that are not only enjoyable—for you and your pet—but which will enhance your dog's agility and training.

Agility competitions/obstacle courses

These exciting activities combine speed and agility, and provide excellent exercise for the dog—and also for the owner. On a typical agility/obstacle course, the dog will have to negotiate hurdles, narrow walkways, ramps, tunnels, and sometimes even water jumps and climbing frames. Highly active small- to medium-size breeds, such as terriers and collies, particularly enjoy these events because they make the most of these animals' natural exuberance, agility, and chasing behaviors.

Dancing competitions

In this sport, the dog performs a choreographed step routine, in response to verbal and hand cues from the owner. Set to music, the routine gives the impression that the animals are dancing.

Obstacle courses offer a great combination of activities that demonstrate your dog's speed and agility, and allow him to make the most of his training.

Flyball competitions

A highly competitive team event carried out against the clock, the dogs must first negotiate a jumping course and then activate a machine that propels a ball into the air. The dog catches the ball, renegotiates the jumps, and races to the finish. Border collies and other highly active dogs with a strong chase instinct excel at this event.

Obedience trials

These events involve many of the activities featured in this book, such as following to heel, off the leash, "sit," "stay," "down," "recall," as well as more advanced techniques such as retrieve. However, at competition level, these activities are conducted to a very high standard.

Working trials

This sport is based on the exercises taught by police dog handlers and other professionals, so it requires a very high standard of training. Dogs are taught to follow a scent track, search for hidden items, retrieve, and follow complicated verbal commands. This kind of activity requires a close partnership between dog and owner that can only be achieved by many hundreds of hours of dedicated training.

Naturally energetic, collies enjoy competition events that appeal to their strength, stamina, and chasing instinct.

7 When and how to ask for advice

One of the best ways to ensure that your puppy stays in good health is to keep a constant eye on his condition. This means not only taking him for routine veterinary examinations, but also checking on his health at home. In this chapter, we show you how to conduct a thorough home health check on your puppy, and we also provide guidelines on first aid, should your puppy be injured or suddenly fall ill. There is also a section on dealing with canine behavioral problems and the benefits of consulting a dog behavior specialist.

Veterinary care

REGULAR VISITS TO THE VETERINARIAN'S OFFICE PLAY A NECESSARY ROLE IN ENSURING YOUR PUPPY'S CONTINUED GOOD HEALTH, BY BOTH PREVENTING AND TREATING DOG AILMENTS AND DISEASES. WITH A LITTLE FORESIGHT, YOU CAN HELP MAKE THESE VISITS LESS STRESSFUL FOR YOUR PET.

A veterinary office can be a frightening place for a puppy. It is filled with strange sights, smells, and people—some dressed in unusual costumes (to a pup, anyway!). If your puppy associates a visit to the veterinarian only with illness, injury, injections, and sometimes pain—and no pleasant experiences at all—the puppy's fear of the place will grow and can stay with him all his life. One way to try to avoid this problem is to take your

Regular routine checkups by a veterinarian can identify potential health problems at an early stage when they are more likely to be successfully treated.

puppy to visit the veterinarian before he has to go for treatment.

In some areas, veterinary practices now hold special open days, or "puppy parties," when owners can take their puppies to meet the veterinarian and the staff in a relaxed and friendly way. Puppies are encouraged to play and to get used to the unusual sights, sounds, and smells. The staff will play with the puppies and handle them, too. When the puppy has to visit the vet for treatment, he will then think of it as a nonthreatening place with nice people who mean him no harm and lots of interesting sensory experiences, and not at all a scary place where strangers only do unpleasant things to him, such as clipping his claws.

You could contact your local vet and ask if the staff organizes open days like this that you can attend. If not, perhaps you could organize your own by asking some other puppy owners to come along with you. If this is not possible, ask if you can visit the office once or twice on your own with your puppy, but make sure they are not too busy. You will need to wait until your puppy has been vaccinated, so contact the vet's office before you go.

Regular home health checks

Puppies are particularly vulnerable to disease, so prompt treatment is vital. The best way to make sure that you spot signs of ill health as soon as

ROUTINE VETERINARY CARE

Your puppy should receive a routine physical examination within 48 hours of purchase to check his general health, so that the puppy can be returned if there is a major problem. This is especially important if the breed is prone to congenital (genetic) disorders. If you are planning to have your pup neutered or spayed, consult your veterinarian early, because opinions differ as to the best age for this to be done. The following medications are usually administered routinely, although some may be given at the discretion of the veterinarian and may depend on the locality and on the incidence of that particular disease in your area.

- Combined distemper-hepatitis-leptospirosis vaccine
- Parvovirus vaccine
- Parainfluenzavirus vaccine
- Rabies vaccine
- Lyme disease vaccine
- Kennel cough vaccine
- Heartworm preventive medication

they appear is to get to know how your puppy looks normally. If you bought your puppy from a reputable breeder, you can be pretty certain that he arrived in the best of health. Note how he looks when he arrives now and examine him regularly, especially during grooming sessions, and you will be able to spot any abnormal changes immediately. For example:

Eyes: Look at the eyeballs and eyelids and check for pink coloration, excess discharge, watering, or sensitivity, which could indicate inflammation due to infection, or a disorder such as an in-growing eyelash.

Ears: Recognize the normal coloring of the inner ears and watch out for unusual odor, discharge, or excess wax.

Mouth: Check the mouth, especially the teeth and gums. Regular toothbrushing should help

ensure good dental health, but it is important to check for tartar buildup, inflammation, and chipped or broken teeth.

Nose: A puppy's nose should be cold and damp. A warm, dry nose—especially if there is any flaking skin—warrants further investigation.

Skin and fur: Regular grooming and preventative medications should help control fleas, ticks, and lice, but it is important to part the puppy's fur and check the skin regularly to look for ticks (especially if your puppy has recently been in wooded areas or other places where deer and other tick-carrying animals live), flaking and scaling, lumps, inflammation, and general irritation and skin sensitivity. In long-haired breeds, check for excess hair around the eyes and matting around the anal region (*see* feeding, page 58, and grooming, page 52) since this can lead to irritation, inflammation, and disease.

Body: Your puppy should be perfectly symmetrical, so any differences in the look and feel of one side of the face or body compared with the other could indicate a swelling or lump due to inflammation or growths. Swollen lymph nodes and/or salivary glands may be a sign of an active infection or other disorder. So check for abnormal swelling below the ears, around the jaw and neck, and around the "armpit" and groin region at the tops of the legs.

Legs and paws: Try observing your puppy when he's walking and running. Look out for limping, whether your puppy is "favoring" a paw, or other signs of an unusual gait. Examine the paws regularly for thorns, splinters, cracking, and bleeding, and any discharge. (*See* page 50 for guidelines on how best to handle and examine your puppy's paws.)

Puppy first aid

Puppies are vulnerable to injury because they are naturally inquisitive, but often don't have the experience to recognize danger. If the injury is serious, seek veterinary care immediately. Calm the puppy by stroking him and talking soothingly while you assess the situation. If the cause of the puppy's injury or distress is not apparent, briefly look for clues but don't delay treatment too long. For example, opened bottles of chemicals, such as pesticides, might indicate poisoning. Close proximity to fields or weedy areas may suggest snake bite or injury caused by another animal. If there is a damaged electrical cable nearby, suspect electrocution. (In this case, switch off the power or use a wooden handle to break the connection, if you can do so safely.) Examine the puppy for inflammation and swelling, especially around the mouth, and also look for bruising, cuts, or other marks. You may notice embedded

Applying an ice pack will help to soothe burns and scalds until you get your puppy to the veterinarian.

stings, skin punctures, or other minor wounds. Seek veterinary help immediately if the injury is serious or the puppy is in distress. The following first-aid measures may, in emergency situations, temporarily ease a puppy's pain and suffering, but don't delay getting professional aid:

Bites and stings: These may cause swelling at the site of the wound. They may be life-threatening if highly toxic or affecting the mouth or throat. Some puppies may be allergic and will react badly. Remove any stings embedded in the wound using tweezers and apply an ice pack to the swelling. Don't approach a snake or other dangerous creature (even if it looks dead) or you may put yourself in danger. (Don't try to remove porcupine quills; leave them for the veterinarian to deal with.)

Burns and scalds: Flush away caustic chemicals using copious amounts of cool water. Apply copious amounts of cold water or an ice pack to burns or scalds for at least ten minutes. Once cool, cover serious burns with a gauze pad and rush to your vet's office at once.

High temperature/hyperthermia: Puppies are most at risk in cars or other vehicles during warm weather or with the heater turned on high. There may be rapid, heavy panting, drooling, weakness, and possible collapse. This is always an emergency requiring prompt first aid and veterinary care. Remove the puppy from the hot environment and reduce his temperature by sponging or spraying with cold (but not ice-cold) water, or by wrapping in damp towels. Apply cold water to prevent the towels from getting too warm. NEVER leave a dog unattended in a car, even with the window partially open. Even in mild weather a car can quickly heat up to a dangerous level.

If your puppy develops hypothermia, wrapping him in a warm towel or blanket will help restore his body temperature.

Minor wounds/bleeding: Bathe the area with warm water containing a suitable antiseptic, and, if necessary, apply a mild antiseptic ointment or cream, as recommended by or obtained from your vet. Never put creams on punctured wounds, no matter how small. They have to be washed off before suturing, causing more tissue damage. Consult your vet if wounds are serious.

Poisoning: Chemical or plant poisons and animal toxins can cause trembling, drooling, vomiting, and possible collapse, and the puppy's pupils may be dilated. There may be swelling around the mouth and throat or around the area of any bite or sting. If you can see the plant or animal responsible, note identifiable features such as shape, size, and coloring so you can describe it later. Always take with you any poison container or plant leaves (if safe to do so) to the vet for identification, and telephone ahead to allow the vet to find out the correct antidote.

Low temperature/hypothermia/frostbite: Puppies most at risk are small or short/smooth-coated breeds in sub-zero temperatures or after immersion in freezing water. Rub the puppy with a thick towel to dry and warm him. Wrap him in a warm towel or blanket (but take care to avoid overheating). Frostbite mainly attacks the extremities such as ears, tail, and feet, which become cold, numb, and pale. Gently massage ears and tail with a warm towel; warm paws in bowls of tepid (not hot) water.

Major wounds/bleeding: Place a pad, ideally made of absorbent gauze (or, in an emergency, use a menstrual pad or your hand) over the wound and apply firm pressure until the bleeding stops. Secure the pad with a bandage and rush to your vet's office immediately.

Puppies suffering from shock should be kept warm and held closely and securely by their owners.

The dog behavior specialist

MANY DOG BEHAVIOR PROBLEMS COME ABOUT BECAUSE OWNERS INTERPRET THEIR PET'S ACTIONS IN HUMAN TERMS RATHER THAN TRYING TO UNDERSTAND CANINE PSYCHOLOGY. IN CASES OF SERIOUS BEHAVIOR PROBLEMS, IT IS ADVISABLE TO CALL IN AN ANIMAL BEHAVIORIST TO UNCOVER THE UNDERLYING CAUSE.

The training program described in this book is specially designed to help prevent a puppy from developing serious behavior problems in the first place. However, despite the owner's best efforts, problems may arise that only an expert can resolve. Some behavior problems, such as hyperactivity, may be due in part to the puppy's diet, especially if he has been fed canned foods that contain a lot of additives. A nutritionist may recommend a change of dietary regimen—and possibly a course of food supplements—that will tackle this issue.

Some problems, such as soiling around the home in the case of a puppy who had been fully house-trained, may indicate an underlying congenital medical condition. This, too, must be checked out by your vet. In other cases, it may be a behavioral problem, often indicating that the puppy is unsettled in some way. Perhaps there has been a major change to his routine, or the arrival of a new member of the household. More complicated behavior problems such as this may require a special training program that only an expert can provide.

Dog trainers can usually offer some advice on tackling behavior problems, or the training school may be able to recommend a suitable specialist. Many veterinarians have an animal behavior expert attached to their practice. Alternatively, ask dog owners you know if they can recommend a suitable expert. Dog behaviorists are known by many different names, including animal psychologists and canine behavior counselors.

Home visit
Depending on the nature of the behavior problem, the expert may be able to find a solution in one consultation, but more often it will require several discussions, some of them on the telephone. The specialist you contact should be prepared to make at least one home visit at a time when the whole family can be present. Most behavior problems can only be understood in the domestic setting, where the specialist can see how the puppy interacts with each member of the household. The animal behaviorist will also take note of how the puppy reacts to him or her as a stranger in the house. Is the puppy relaxed and welcoming, or timid and fearful? Is the pup demanding and attention-seeking, or does he lie down quietly when asked?

Right relationships
The specialist will establish whether any area of the relationship between the puppy and the human family needs attention. Some problem behaviors can be innate. Hounds naturally chase, herding dogs often want to run and round up people and other animals, and terriers dig and explore every leaf and crevice. The specialist will have advice on ways to channel these natural behaviors into less antisocial activities.

Consistency problems

It is also important to know who looks after the puppy and the kind of training program that has been followed. The whole family should take part in a discussion about the puppy's handling and training to ensure that everyone is following the same approach. Problems can occur simply because of a lack of consistency in the way commands or the "house rules" are applied, leading to confusion and distress in the puppy. The puppy's daily routine and the amount of mental stimulation he receives can have a direct bearing on behavior as well. Therefore the expert will need to discuss how much time the owners spend with him in training and play.

The specialist will be interested to know of any alterations in the domestic environment that may have brought about your puppy's problem behavior. Puppies are very sensitive to changes in the household, such as the appearance of a new baby, the presence of new guests staying at the house, a new pet, a house move, a divorce, or even arguments between family members. It may be that the puppy's main care provider has

recently started a new job and the puppy is now being left unattended for longer periods than he had been used to.

Socialization problems

It is also important to make sure that the puppy is thoroughly socialized (see page 126), both with people and other dogs. An overly friendly dog who is scolded for being too boisterous with strangers may associate the stranger with the reprimand, rather than his own behavior, and come to distrust all visitors. It is better if the puppy is taught the correct way to behave when meeting new people, such as sitting quietly beside his owner and waiting for the stranger to make a fuss over him. In the park, before being allowed off the leash to play with other dogs, the puppy should be encouraged to wait for his owner's permission to join his friends—perhaps with a "sit" or "watch me"—rather than rushing off as soon as he is released. By using this method, you can prevent the problem of a puppy that tends to run off immediately after every dog he sees or encounters.

The authors, Maggie Holt (left) and Stella Sweeting (right) with their well-trained and happy family of canine friends.

Index